Small Talk . . .

Memories of an Edwardian Childhood

NAOMI MITCHISON

Small Talk . . .

Memories of an Edwardian
Childhood

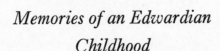

THE BODLEY HEAD

LONDON   SYDNEY
TORONTO

For
the grand-daughters,
who ask questions

© Naomi Mitchison 1973
Photographs © Naomi Mitchison 1973
ISBN 0 370 10490 0
Printed and bound in Great Britain for
The Bodley Head Ltd
9 Bow Street, London WC2E 7AL
by W & J Mackay Limited, Chatham
Set in 'Monotype' Imprint
First published 1973

CONTENTS

ILLUSTRATIONS

FOREWORD

The table on the next page shows relationships. My first Oxford home was 11 Crick Road, but I don't remember it at all. Then we were at 4 St Margaret's Road and finally at Cherwell, which had a different status, more satisfactory I expect to my mother. It was more like a miniature estate at the bottom of Linton Road, then a thick-hedged lane with open meadows on three sides of it. Another version of the years about which I write comes into the later chapters of my mother's book, *Friends and Kindred*. Hers and mine have a different social and political bias. If the rest of the family ever start on the same thing theirs will be different again. And so the whirligig of time brings in his revenges.

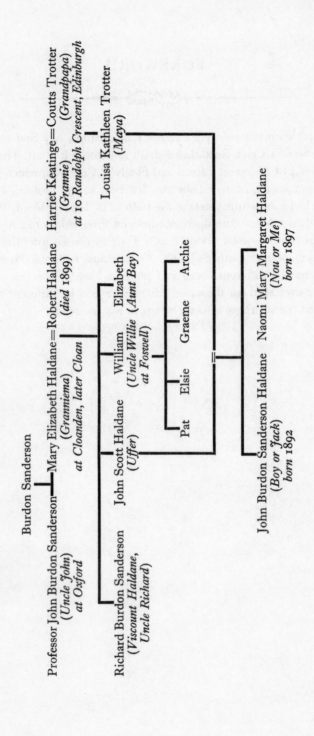

I

Becoming Oneself

It was bright and bobbing. Out of my dark cave I reached for it. My hands wavered up to it. It came nearer. Did I catch it? The importance was the attempt. My brother's long fair hair was cut before he was six years old, which means that I, under the hood of my pram, was under a year old. But me.

Then I had a mail-cart made of brown cane instead of a pram. I sat in it. Nobody made me lie down. True, there was a strap but it had a grown-up type buckle. No shawls or blankets but instead horrid gaiters with buttons which always pinched my legs. Sometimes (or perhaps once) grown-ups, speaking of me in my mail-cart, called it a pram. I became terribly indignant. My new status had been denigrated: how could I bear it? Certainly I couldn't explain. I think I screamed. Status—essential for all gregarious animals, essential in the farmyard. Now I knew it and would always know it.

Everyone went to Studland, a suitable place for a young and not highly pecunious upper-middle-class family from Oxford. I have no idea where we stayed but there was a large object up on a cliff round which I ran in a somewhat ritual manner because I was frightened of it. Why? Well, I was frightened of a lot of things and today it is not clear how these things were related. I did not speak of them except on the very rare occasions when terror drove me into hysterical screaming. It was quite clear to me at the time that if I told anyone 'They' would make it a lot worse for me. 'They' who appeared in dreams and in triangular shapes which I recognised with alarm in Gabon metal work many years later and in obvious reds and purples. 'They.' Are other people's 'They' like mine?

'They' said if you choose
To boil eggs in your shoes . . .

And, oh, that was what I always did! Tell me, do your 'They'
allow you to do offbeat things? Or on the contrary, do 'They'
insist that you do them?

But apart from that we went down to the beach by what was
either a tunnel or an overgrown green lane. I think there were
bathing boxes or tents. My mother floated in a long white cotton
gown; she never could swim but float she did in very shallow water
and I perambulated her fluttering wet edges.

The dresses which my mother wore on dry land would have
been extremely fashionable today. There was a splendid silvery
brocade with mauve and green thistles, no doubt worn for best
Oxford dinner parties, cut low; there was much lace and an infra-
structure of whale-boned stays built by her *corsetière*, and longish
white bloomers. Never to my knowledge did I see her wearing less,
though she did, I understand, suckle me for nine months. She wore
opaque black cotton stockings; the best of them had silk clocks.
Her mother, on the other hand, had white ones of finer cotton or
even silk. My two grandmothers dressed differently. Grannie, my
mother's mother, *née* Keatinge, was, I suspect, rather expensively
dressed with foamings and flouncings of lace, black or white, and
really beautiful and romantic caps of lace and broad satin ribbons.
For all this a lady's maid was essential. But Granniema, my Haldane
grandmother, would not exactly have had a lady's maid. Indeed,
this might have savoured of Tory episcopalianism. Probably the
upper housemaid washed her smalls, sewed and mended, though
perhaps Baba, who had been nurse to my father's generation, did a
bit of that after her charges grew up, she having accurately foretold
their future careers. Baba lived in a special little room in the older
and prettier part of Cloan and sometimes asked us children to tea
there. We had to behave. But the one I remember at Cloan, who
was always called a maid-companion and did not wear uniform,
was Irving, always referred to by her surname and not to be mis-
taken for a servant. One had therefore to be very much aware of the

social boundaries and not to make mistakes. Granniema wore stiff black; her caps tended to have violets and small fountains of jet and she had a shining black stick. As children, we were rather frightened of her, but she became more and more of a friend.

I doubt if either grandmother would have gone to Studland; did they go away for holidays except to other people's houses? If so, I guess it would have been to a reputable resort, perhaps in Germany or France, a place where one might take the waters and go to an occasional good concert of serious music. One awkward thing about Studland was that there were trippers. What they were like has vanished, but, dreadfully, I did once find myself in some form of social contact. What? No, that has vanished, but I remember my mother speaking to me very seriously about my *faux pas*. Guilt was duly aroused, though I never knew quite what I had done. This, however, was the beginning of class-consciousness.

That curious word 'tripper', probably right out of the current vocabulary! It dates from the time when most people could only afford a few days' holiday but when they did they came irritatingly into the very same places which those who could afford longer holidays had claims on and when they got there they made uncouth noises and wore unsuitable townee clothes. Perhaps one notices a touch of the same feeling among the conservation-minded today. The word disappears; the feelings remain.

Meanwhile, I was being taught to read by my mother at home. It was a phonetic system and at four I had no bother with cat, mat and sat but suddenly I was confronted with four-letter words. A feeling overwhelmed me that I would never be able to understand, never. I have had that feeling since: about economics, about physics and, oddly, about lawn tennis. These were all things I wanted to be competent at, but felt deep down I couldn't do. Other subjects I was either good at or didn't particularly want to understand or else felt that I could if I took trouble—and sometimes did. But this dead-end feeling is unmistakable. On this first occasion it was clearly infuriating to my maternal teacher. She spanked me hard and I was put into my cot, the nursery curtains were drawn and I was left to think it over as soon as I had stopped howling. It hadn't really hurt. The offence was to my human dignity. I did not forgive it. But it made me understand how other people feel about affronted human dignity. This has been useful. It was also useful because suddenly I was able to read not only words of four letters but all words. Unhappily I never got a sufficient jolt over economics or physics.

As far as I remember my main punishment as a child was not being smacked but being told that I was 'hurting Mother'. If one was disobedient—and this was rubbed in from early readings of Kipling's *Jungle Book* which put a great emphasis on obedience as did, I think, Montefiore's *Bible for Home Reading*—or told lies or was in any way treacherous, it hurt Those who Loved One Most. Let me add that this was not a God-centred household; we were brought up as highly moral agnostics. It never occurred to me that it was treachery to conceal my fears and secret propitiations of 'Them' which sometimes involved things like knocking my head against the bars of my cot for a specified number of times.

But I do remember the first time I got away with a lie. There was a large tea-party with my favourite goodies: those little cakes with marshmallow inside and chocolate on top. I was tempted. A plate was discovered with one missing. I denied it passionately and with tears; at last I was believed or possibly it was thought better that I should appear to be believed. In general I wasn't much of a liar. In fact, I was a fairly good little girl and I was allowed to do a reasonable amount of physically dangerous things like climbing trees and rocks, running along the garden wall and of course, when the time came and I was five years old, going to school across Banbury Road, a thing which no parent would allow a child to do in today's Oxford. But then the main traffic was still the horse trams which one could race, always catching up at the stops.

I got away with a lie later on when I suppose I was seventeen or eighteen and my father inadvertently opened an indiscreet love letter addressed to my brother whose initials were the same as his own—something every family should avoid. My father became very much upset and I took a deep breath and jumped right in, explaining that I knew the lady in question and she was all that could be desired and so on. I had no idea who she was but knew I must protect my brother and by that time knew something of the art of fiction. Again I was either believed or appeared to be believed and was given the letter to forward.

Yet surely, surely, I must have told lies dozens of times between these two? Or did each of them mark a step in sophistication, perhaps in liberation, and so become memorable?

One of the nicest things about my young life was my mice. After breakfast I changed into my mouse frock or perhaps pinafore—dark blue it was—and the darling silky mice came out of their cage and wandered over me: I don't know how or why we communicated but presumably we did. Sometimes the mice climbed down me on to the floor and I after them. How pleasing and how large things are from underneath! But there are sadly too many edges and corners on the level of one's head. Being close to the ground gives one a delicious intimate view of flowers, the fine structure of stones and earth and half peeled sticks, and in those days the muddy bottoms of one's elders' skirts.

I spent, as all children do in all cultures, part of my life on my own and part on the fringes of adult culture. As soon as I could be guaranteed not to make awkward remarks or fidget unendurably I was taken out calling. This meant hiring a landau, an open carriage with a small seat opposite the big one, but nicer because nearer the rushing ground, and going the rounds of academic Oxford, leaving the right number of cards and congratulating ourselves when those we called on were 'not at home'. The driver too used to turn round and felicitate us. Later, as we rose in the social scale, we had two carriages of our own and a hard-mouthed mare. For these expeditions I wore white cotton frillies, with broad blue ribbons to match my eyes, catching back my long pale gold hair, and a sun-hat. The difficulty was that these hats tended to be tethered by elastics which were likely to bite one.

At five I wore bunchy white cotton frocks well down below the knee, the neck frill outlined with red cross-stitch. One of these now is in the Langley Moore Collection in Bath. I don't remember finding this interfered with my activities, but my big wish was always for bare feet and sandals, not socks and shoes, and I disapproved of some of the Flower Fairies in my favourite book, who even wore boots.

My mother certainly had a parasol, black and white, not coloured which would have been vulgar, or even 'fast'. The carriage went at no more than a slow trot, so that the parasol did not blow away but could stay up. The sun was not yet directly welcomed. She would have worn one of her best hats, muslin on a wire frame, with fairly simple flowers or perhaps ostrich feathers. She would not wear any feathers for which birds were specially killed. I think she must have been a beautiful woman at this time, though rather severe-looking; do children make these aesthetic judgements? She never made up, but occasionally, if she was hot and flushed, used *papier poudré*, which came in little books, and mopped up any unseemly damp, after which it left the cheeks and nose delicately pale.

If we were unlucky enough to find someone 'in' I would be allowed to look round the room with my hands behind my back, a habit I still find myself continuing in museums. Many of our friends had curios, some of great fascination. Many ended up in the Pitt Rivers Museum or the Ashmolean, as indeed some of my parents' curios have done. When we got back home we rushed to see who had called on us. The parlour maid would duly have laid out the cards on a Benares brass tray. This ritual involved some deception, but all for the good cause of upper-middle-class solidarity. I call it upper-middle-class which seems to me historically correct. But we would certainly have called ourselves 'upper class'. Now, if I am asked, I shy away and call myself a 'clerc' or use the rather unpleasing phrase 'professional class' which was not current earlier in the century.

At this time we lived at 4 St Margaret's Road in a detached house of its period, remarkably ugly. There was a great big brass knob on the front door, a circular space in front which we called a drive, and a wide wooden gate on which I was not supposed to swing, with almond trees at both sides. There was also a basement with kitchen, scullery, a servants' WC. Was there perhaps also a servants' bedroom? I was not encouraged to explore, either by parents or servants, though sometimes an amiable cook would let me have bits of dough to make biscuits. The whole basement was dark, lit from a front area which enclosed the windows almost totally and a back area with a slope of rubble or stone on the garden side. One could climb down into this and here my brother and I used to lay trains of gunpowder and have small explosions, sometimes singeing our hair or eyelashes. On the ground floor you went through to the garden; the stairs went straight up and down. There was a largish drawing-room, a study, a dining-room, perhaps a pantry at the head of the back stairs down to the basement, and certainly a gentleman's lavatory. All this was standard in a detached house of the period. There were, rather surprisingly, two bathrooms, one of them rather scruffy, and there was also a water closet with a bottom pan opening down into darkness and smell. This probably induced constipation in everybody. I find, from my mother's book, that they put in the second bathroom; my father had a theory that ordinary baths did not conduct the heat properly so our baths must be made of lead. This certainly warmed up, but was rather cheerless and needed a lot of special cleaning.

The house was lit by gas and from my cot I could see above the nursery screen the pale crocus of dim light and the nasty shadows which could be chased away when some grown-up turned it full on into a bright fish-tail. My father, who was one of the Metropolitan Gas Referees, keeping constant check from the London office which he visited every week on the quality of coal-gas, did not think too well of it and we all had a healthy distrust of leaks and were very careful about turning things on and off. However, we moved to a non-gas house, Cherwell, at the end of Linton Road which at that time ended as a thick-hedged lane, when I was nine. I loved being able to flick on an electric light switch but my mother, in the interests of economy, only had rather low candle-power bulbs in passages, bathrooms and so on, and everything had to be turned off by the last person going to bed.

Talking of my parents' curios, there was a very handsome large scarab which was the pride of their Egyptian collection. Looking at it when I took over the estate, I was doubtful. When I went along with it to the British Museum they, while happily accepting various duller looking bits and pieces, asked me if I could date its acquisition into the family. Knowing when my grandfather went on the Grand Tour (a letter from Lord Cockburn of 1854 dates this) I told them. They were delighted; it was the earliest forgery they had ever met!

II

Real and Not Real

To look at, the doll's house is a solid white cupboard but with windows at the sides. When you unlock it there are six rooms all the same size; from the very beginning they were kitchen, dining-room; one up, drawing-room and best bedroom; two up, nursery and schoolroom. But the furniture is anything but to scale and, alas, in the course of being played with, a lot of it has gone and almost all the Hubbard household, which is very sad. Mrs Hubbard had a china face and hands, as well as feet in black boots and a lovely lilac silk dress; she usually lay on the sofa where I could see her boots. The solid Goan carved chairs and table are still there, too big for the rest, but where is the ivory *chaise percée* and where the work table with its tiny scissors and balls of silk?

In those days, as a literal-minded small girl, I was worried both by the awkwardness of scale and by the problem of the fourth wall. I could pretend that there were other rooms and stairs at the back but I found it very hard to make the open rooms look 'real'. Nor do most doll's furnishings have attractive or well finished backs. I have done a bit of refurnishing since those days but most modern things are too small and flimsy. Nor is there any place for today's bathroom fittings; there used to be a gentleman's hip bath, the kind my mother's father insisted on having in front of the fire in his bedroom long after the Edinburgh house had a bathroom. Duly pails were carried up. My doll's house hot-water can seems to have gone too. It was like the little brass ones that used to be found sitting, a hot towel over them, on one's washstand at suitable times—they were pretty and comforting and someone else emptied the basin of dirty water, while one was out of the room. However, I still have one doll's house washstand with a basin and ewer. People who came to visit my parents often brought me doll's house presents. That little jug came from Niels Bohr, those wooden kitchen things including a churn from an Austrian physiologist—but who? Most of the *décor* dates back to my mother's childhood.

But I was too much of a realist and too little theatre-minded to enjoy it wholeheartedly. How far can realism go? When I cut open one of my dolls, dribbled the contents into a small cauldron and heated it on—real?—imaginary?—flames I can remember my disappointment that it still wasn't edible. My brother and I between us skinned a furry caterpillar for a rug, but it shrivelled up. So many things ought to have worked but didn't. As well perhaps to learn this young.

Once at a picnic up the Cherwell, where we usually went on Sundays and always made a fire for the tea kettle, I simply had to walk through the lovely soft shimmering grey ashes. How delicious they were going to feel on my bare skin! But of course it wasn't like that at all; I still remember the scorch pattern on my feet between the sandal straps.

I do however remember clearly that the goldfish inside the great Famille Rose Chinese bowl that once stood in the corner of the Edinburgh drawing-room used to swim round and eat the crumbs I put in. Sadly these same goldfish are now only painted on the inside of the bowl. This kind of memory makes one just a little uncertain of others. The butterfly that I tamed? Throwing the milk off the tray of my high chair? Probably I did, but I hardly think I can remember it. Or again, that piece of radium my brother convinced me that he had in his desk? And surely he once let me see it sparkling inside a dark cupboard?

I am quite sure all the same about our railway which we had in an empty and no doubt unattractive room at the top of the house. Every birthday or Christmas saw more rails or more trucks. We sent off the clockwork trains, timing them so that they did—or didn't—miss one another on loops which we had constructed. It was terribly exciting being at the points and knowing that the lives of the trains depended on one. Sometimes if we were quite sure we had arranged a train smash, we would put night lights inside the carriages and turn out the lights. That made it all the better. My brother was five years older than me but I tried so hard to keep up and often succeeded.

We had two splendid boxes of bricks, hard-wood with straight edges, cut to size. With these we built mostly castles and forts which we garrisoned with our lead soldiers and then fired at with spring-loaded artillery whose wooden projectiles could make a real dent, in time bringing the whole thing satisfactorily crashing down. For further realism, we sometimes put in cotton-wool soaked in methylated spirits which our mother used for her curling tongs, and lighted it. We were probably safer with naked flames than today's switch-on—switch-off children.

Things seemed to be always cheerful and in the everyday world with my brother Jack—Boy for me. Certainly he did testing things sometimes like making the water in the basin live—off the ordinary house electricity when we finally got it—and putting in pennies for me to snatch. Often he teased me till my temper went and I stamped and screamed, feeling furiously helpless. I hated him for minutes and then suddenly it was all over. But this wasn't the kind of thing which really worried me. This was alive. What I was afraid of was not alive. It was what lay behind the apparent silence and stillness of inanimate objects, including bed knobs, roof finials and the pigeon house—not the pigeons.

There were so many propitiations to go through in my daily life. When I was dressed and my hair brushed and I came down to the drawing-room for tea I used to have to look at the de Morgan tiles and say, 'I'm afraid that hoopoe will eat my dolly'. After that it was all right. The hoopoe still looked fierce but its soul was safely locked into the tile. Nor did I worry much about my dolly which I have now quite forgotten; I was never particularly maternal about them. This propitiation was public; but it was not public that there was a certain chair which I always avoided touching. It was a high-backed *art nouveau* piece and in the end attained a good cash value so I sold it into slavery, getting even with it more than half a century later. The grandfather clocks were equally ominous and likely to become animated, but I put this down to the story someone told me about a clock that ate (or chased) a little boy. This animation of the inanimate strikes me as basically terror-making. At one time I was constantly being taken into old furniture or curiosity shops and kept on having to jump round to see what the chairs, mirrors or suits of armour were up to. I thoroughly hated any story that had this as part of it, and if I was ever asked to a rather grand Christmas party my mother had to make sure there wasn't going to be a ventriloquist, as she knew from dire experience that if there was she might have to take me back screaming and probably wetting my drawers.

Mirrors—looking-glasses (I know that one was a more powerful word than the other, but which?—it was nothing to do with U or non-U), were especially treacherous, most of all tall ones with claw legs like the one in the St Margaret's Road drawing-room which one was aware of even from outside, passing the small window. But I didn't like even the smallest. In all the fairy tales, including George MacDonald's *Phantastes*, which affected me deeply with its concern about beauty and guilt, mirrors were not to be trusted. They told too much or too little. I wrote most of them out of my system in an early verse play.

Of course there were areas of safety; nothing could get at me if I curled up on my father's lap, holding on to his ear with one thumb tucked into it. He had a big brown moustache and a wide Haldane nose with a small lump on it which I liked. When he kissed me it was rough and tickly. Across his front was a gold watch chain with a big tick-tock watch on the end. In my own children's time it also had a chocolate tree which flowered into silver-paper covered chocolates. All about him was safe. And there were areas of laughter and excitement, especially a long saga Boy told me about a family like ourselves and they went along and they went along and suddenly they met—perhaps—a bear and something shatteringly funny always happened. I was a plump little girl and these gales of laughter were quite painful, one felt one was going to come in two. It was almost as shattering as being teased. He was at the Dragon School where I too would go when I was five and the characters in the story were called with exquisite humour the Wagons. That always set us both off. Later on the story had three canoes called The Vagus, The Cornucopia and The Little Mary; but this was a stage on in sophistication.

But there were also lots of ordinary games. The main one, any time, was some form of hide-and-seek. There is a family story of my father bringing back a plague rat from the Lister Institute in a paper bag and leaving it in his overcoat pocket. The hat and coat stand in the front hall was one of my favourite hiding places and I can remember my indignation at being hauled out by a grown-up who wasn't in the game.

My nurse was called Sina; perhaps there had been others before her but she was the only one I remember. When she went away for her holiday she always sent me country butter in a blue cup. Once I wrote to thank her, saying I would soon have a tea set, but my mother told me this was wrong, it looked as if I expected to get more, and perhaps also she didn't like me to be too fond of Sina, whom I now remember as someone who was always nice to me, perhaps because 'a servant' would never be allowed to punish me. She was still there when I first went to school and for several years after that; she comes into my earlier diaries, but I think she must have left in late 1907 when we moved to Cherwell and before I broke my leg. It would have been a good thing if she could have been with me after that instead of some of the professional nurses whom I so hated.

Food in those days was still nursery food. One wasn't allowed for instance cheese, bacon or fried potatoes. There was not so much raw fruit as now, except what we acquired by our own wits. My mother in any case refused to have onions in her house. Much later, when I occasionally cooked for her, I introduced a small amount, particularly in curries which she liked because of Kipling and her romantic view of India, clear in her own book, and she always enjoyed the 'Indian' flavour I had so cleverly put in. Breakfast was porridge, probably a boiled egg and milk. Lunch tended to be stew, cottage pie, tasteless boiled cod with a small pool of egg sauce, and so on, but roast beef on Sundays. There would be milk pudding afterwards, though we did have castle puddings and big fruit pies—not flans which came in much later. On week-days we often had boiled salt beef with carrots; I hated that. Sometimes there were boiling fowls with lumpy white sauce over macaroni. Roast chicken was birthday food. Cooking was much less interesting and varied than it is today. Tea was bread and butter, bread and jam, cake. Biscuits were not as common as they are now; there were none that came my way with chocolate or sugary fillings, but we did have alphabet biscuits and in Scotland 'squashed flies'. There seemed almost always to be an evening spoonful of cod liver oil or something of the kind. Milk was always boiled and I hated it. In spite of this boiled milk I got TB and swollen neck glands which were painted with iodine. I had to wear a collar to cover them.* There must have been other treatments as well, for I remember various doctors poking me and muted quarrels between my father and mother. Finally the glands were operated on and I came out of the nursing home with a nasty scar about which I was very conscious. But at least on TB I was negative.

But there was constant winter illness of a vague kind, coughs and cough mixtures, being sick and having nightmares. Sina slept beside me. But sometimes she didn't wake and the nightmare went on in the dark even though I seemed to be awake myself. I heard the trains hooting in the distance and sometimes the beat of horse hooves but of course never a car. The blinds were drawn down and I waited and waited until, as Stevenson said, 'day shall be blue on the window blind'. Of course there was also standard measles and my brother pretending I was a lion and feeding me through the bars of the cot. It left me with a nice long word: photophobia. There was chicken pox and horrible whooping cough that went on

* My 1905 (seven years old) diary says: 'After breakfast Dr Hale White took me to an instrument maker to be measured for a collar, which he and Sir Alfred Fripp proscribed to keep my glands still. I have got the collar on now, and I have to have my writing proped up because I cannot bend my head forward, so I am afraid my writing is worse than usual. At the instrument maker's I saw an operating sofa where you were X-rayed.'

All quotations from the diaries are *verbatim*.

and on. Illness was something one took for granted and was nothing to do with the terrors of fantasy or the other sharp terror, that one's mother might—some day—die.

Purges were usual for anything and fiercely effective: calomel or castor oil. There were also enemas; any psychologist will point out the deleterious effects of the latter as a punishment fantasy. A few household remedies survive from those days: some quite effective cough mixtures, Eno's and Dr Collis Browne's chlorodyne. But the real jump came first with sulfonamides and then with the antibiotics. We fussed much more about cleanliness at an earlier time. It seems likely that sterilising instruments for an operation was more necessary; one couldn't afford an infection—the kind of thing which is so quickly dealt with now. Iodine always went on cuts; one had to be brave. But doctors came to the house and of course treated us all for nothing, as doctors at that time always did for one another's families. My father had actually been a practising doctor in the wards of the Royal Infirmary at Edinburgh and I think he still felt that bleeding was a good thing though it was never practised on any of us.

But blood was interesting and something to do with physiology —that long word!—and the lab where one could play with fascinating things including of course the original Haldane gas analysis apparatus and those lovely little blobs of mercury that one could chase right across the floor.

By that time my father had done his classic work on sewer gas, mostly in the Dundee sewers, where he knew by the smell of raw jute or bitter oranges which factory effluents were coming in. Now he was working on the physiology of breathing, writing scientific papers alone or in collaboration, but also writing on the philosophical concepts which arose from this work. But it was always solidly based on the experiments which were going on, some of which, rightly and properly, were on himself. He was a Fellow of New College, conscientiously interested in College problems, and usually dined in Hall on Sundays. I grew out of childhood into a healthy respect for scientific curiosity and work, but I never had my brother's early understanding of it, and I wonder, now, whether this was temperamental or whether certain avenues of understanding were closed to me by what was considered suitable or unsuitable for a little girl. Not deliberately closed, I think, since both my parents believed in feminine emancipation, but— there is a difference between theory and practice.

III

The Evidence

There are two ways of writing this kind of book. One is by an act of acute remembrance, sometimes by concentrating on some small object, some tail-end which may, so to speak, be hauled on until the whole animal is revealed. Again, dreams may help, though they may also worry and obscure; one must be careful. A place re-visited, although it may have been almost completely changed, still keeps something which will start up the memory train. The smell of gas, the smell of drains, the smell of old-fashioned roses or mignonette, the smell of stables, these can be starters.

But I have something else of a very definite kind. First of all there are the diaries of the summer holidays, which all pupils of the Dragon School were expected to keep, though no doubt not all the juniors did. My mother had ours bound. There they are. Mine date from 1904 (Naomi Haldane age six—Form 1). There are three of my brother's, from 1902 on. The last was written at eleven. At twelve he was doubtless preparing for Eton. We always got prizes for our diaries and no wonder, or so I say now; we were both highly literate. So I can use these to check my memories. Or can I? I try to remember the actual process of writing. 'Have you done your diary?' It was not a welcome activity. Since then I have kept diaries at various periods of stress in my life, including the years of the last war. But these were partly therapeutic, to calm down some of my troubles, or even solve them, by writing about them. These early diaries were holiday tasks with emphasis on the last word.

They are all written on paper with double lines ruled faint. In many ways the handwriting gets worse and worse, curiously more like my brother's which was notoriously bad, though no doubt it went quicker over the years. They are all illustrated, mostly with flowers, though I try people, not very successfully, at a later stage. My brother's illustrations are practically all plans and diagrams. He always refers to his 'pater & mater'. When did that stop? There are picture postcards, but not the photos which one would expect today's children to use. On the other hand in the 1909 diary when I was eleven, there are two or three pencil drawings of considerable aesthetic demerit—let me say quickly!—which recall vividly the dress and even attitudes of train travellers of this date. In my early diaries I was clearly hampered by having to use either crayons or unsatisfactory water colours. But in the 1904 diary at six, there is a drawing of a barley ear which I do remember doing because it was the first time I had really looked at the shape of a barley ear and the twist of the leaf and it was deeply absorbing. A few of these pictures recall their making and the taste of the paint when one accidentally sucked one's brush. There is one of bees on a flower of *buddleia globosa*. There was a big (to me) bush of this in the left-hand bottom corner of the St Margaret's Road garden.

But the content of the diaries? Can I fairly use these for checking my own memories or should they be set down straight without passing through the memory sieve? Clearly the memories, as they come into consciousness sixty or sixty-five years later (sometimes more), have been distorted and censored. There is an element of subconscious choice. But equally there is an element of choice in the diaries, which are all about outside events in the sense that all the ghosts and terrors have been eliminated. I would not have written about those under any compulsion; I doubt if a psychiatrist could have got them out of me, though perhaps careful watching of my play activities might have revealed something. But fear was shameful, and to speak or write might bring 'Them' to life.

So what? Let us see. Page 1, July 23 1904: 'After dinner Boy and Baines went on the River, & Mother & I went to see Miss Northcroft off, & to buy a boat hook. Then we went to Worcester to feed the swans, we found some, & some cygnets. The cygnets were grey, with almost grey beaks & feet; some of them had feather sheaths still on their young feathers. The swans & ducks fed out of our hands, & one swan bit a hole in my thumb. Some boys were fishing close by, & the fish came for the bread which we gave the swans. We had gooseberries & sponge cake for tea which we had under a horsechestnut-tree. We saw a Thrush which was hitting a snailshell against the parth, so as to get the snail out, to eat it.'

The next day the family went on the river. 'We saw a lot of Arrowhead, & flowering-Rush & goldenrod & lithram & Epilobiun & Water Lilies, yelow & white, & creeping-jenny, & tansy in flower. We had dinner in a fairly nettly field, & afterwards Boy bathed, with a fairly good effect. Then we paddled, & got plenty of Plantorbises; they are like flat snail-shells. Then we went home.'

This shows a remarkable degree of observation and the power to write it down,* though I don't much care for so many commas. Clearly I must have asked for a lot of the spellings, but equally clearly I made an attempt at some of them which didn't always come off. I was well used to Latin botanical names though sometimes I got the spelling wrong and didn't know loose-strife or willow-herb. This also shows that flowering rush, now rare, was common only a mile or so up the Cherwell where one no longer finds much in the way of flowers. Over the 'plantorbises', I was keeping up with my elders!

I know that, when I wrote my diary, I was encouraged to describe things I had seen; often I would pick up the words of the grownups. But sometimes I rush off on my own. When the British Medical Association came to Oxford 'Mr Lorrain-Smith gave me this:

> 'An owl and a pussy-cat came to me
> In a beautiful rocking boat
> They took some honey
> But I couldent see the money
> In a barrel with on it wrote
> Honey

* My brother's diary says: 'I got some fairly good specimens of *Planorbis corneus, Paludina vivipara, Limnaea auriculata,* & *Anodonta anatina.* N.B. This year I am going to make Naomi write all the botany, as she is far better at it than I am. We met a good few other chaps up the river.'

All this was made of wood,
And on the grass it stood.
And besides that a mouse-trap that
works with a spring.'

And now I can clearly picture the otherwise forgotten owl and
pussycat, a wooden toy balancing on a bar with a weighted rod below
which made it swing. My finger went out to rock it, often, often.

Sentiment breaks in, 'some dear little pigs', 'a dear little puppy,
he was quite brown, though his mother was white and black! his
teeth all except the canines were as small as my teeth when I was a
baby.' Food is important. 'We found a great many Dewberries, so
many we could not eat them all.' There are books which I read:
The Stokesley Secret, Hiawatha, The Treasure Seekers. But I seem
to make few literary comments, in my early diaries at least.

In fact the diaries are, very properly, extroverted. It is only from
further away that I can see inside the child. The diary writer sees
people through their achievements. In my seven-year-old diary:
'We met Prof D'Arcy Thompson who knows more about whales
than anybody else in the world.'

How, then, should I use them now? I can scarcely mix them in,
unless a chance word or two brings back a scene or even a state of
mind so vividly that it becomes part of adult memory. The fairest
thing to do, perhaps, is to add the diaries' comments separately.

What a bore it was to have to get down to writing the day's page,
chivvied into it, often at the spare writing table in the Cloan
drawing-room which had a very ornate black, cast-iron ink-
stand with two inkwells, various pens and a sheet of white blotting
paper which one was not supposed to draw on. There were also two
short, also rather ornate, silver candlesticks, for sealing, and there
may well have been one of the many silver trowels, suitably in-
scribed, which Uncle Richard was given after laying foundation
stones.

Maya collected the written sheets (occasionally making me re-
write those which had been hopelessly blotted) which otherwise
would have escaped. In the diaries she is always, more formally,

Mother, though in those years I did not think of her like that. But the fact that she read what I had written and that I wanted so much to please her, may account for some of my sentiments. These were second-hand, but my observations on natural history and, occasionally, industrial processes, were genuine, and when I wrote that something was lovely (I didn't use many other praise words) it is probable that I genuinely thought so.

But there are also quite a lot of letters. I turned a bundle of these over to the Edinburgh Central library with various other documents which had started heavily accumulating in the house, and happily forgot all about them. The early letters are in rather worse spelling than the diaries, more blotchy, but full of life. There are some from my brother and one from my father to him, which had somehow got into the bundle. I think my mother must have kept all our childhood letters; some are dated in her hand, especially those from my brother at five or six, sometimes with a proud note they were written without help. In one, to her, he slightly complains: 'Nou wants so much looking after when you're away.' However, I kept myself busy; one of the earlier letters encloses lots of empty seed packets which I had sowed in my own garden, a square in the bottom bed of the St Margaret's Road garden. This was always rather disappointing; they never quite looked like the pictures on the outside of the packet.

There are a number from Jack to me, signed Boydie, which was my baby version of Boy dear. He expected me to understand and sympathise with what he was after. A 1906 letter, when I was eight, tells me in detail about how well he was likely to do in 'Trials' and what prizes he hoped to win. By that time he must have come to terms with Etonian savagery and was determined to get what he could out of the place.

Sometimes the letters recall a definite memory. One from Cornwall is about elvers climbing up a waterfall, and now, reading it, I remember the dark green, wet, hanging, slippery, glancing things. Now and then they recall another name from school days or some specially good ploy. How lucky that I didn't know I was going to re-read them so many years later in so different a world.

Finally, there is my mother's book of memoirs, *Friends and Kindred*. The later chapters overlap the period about which I am writing. She was fifteen years older than I am now when she started writing them, largely at my daughter's and my own instigation. I have gone back from time to time to her book and, so to speak, checked with her, sometimes with a touch of subliminal argument.

IV

Cloan

How cold it was getting out at Auchterarder station! It had been
a wearisome journey up, with the wait and change at Rugby, a long
gloomy platform. But on the next session we had splendid iron
foot-warmers filled with boiling water put into our compartment.
Was it a night journey, waking in Scotland and another change, I
think, at Larbert? Or did things work out (perhaps when we went
over from Edinburgh) so that we got to Auchterarder in the late
afternoon and there was a carriage waiting for us with the two
horses stamping and tossing their heads? It smelt of straw and
fustiness and those with a keen nose would tell every time one of
the pair of horses lifted her tail. But as we got up a little, crossing
the burn at the stone bridge, the smell sharpened with the scent of
pine needles and beech leaves and the horses went slower. As we
came through the gate the sound of the hooves and wheels changed
and went squashier and grittier as we got on to the gravel drive. I
pulled down a window. The leaves rustled; there were sounds
different from Oxford. We got to the house and the faintly lit
windows high up and the porch and the wall thick with jasmine,
then the lights streaming out of the wide door, the horses pulling
up and Aunt Bay waiting for us with open arms.

Cloanden (as it was then, but by 1904 Uncle Richard had begun
to change the name back to the original Cloan) is half way up the
Ochills with a splendid northwest view across Strathearn into the
Highlands. It was originally a pleasant little farmhouse with the
traditional square of buildings at the back, byres and stables, sheds
and bothies. But gradually in the course of the nineteenth century
it was built on to, first an enormously inconvenient spiral staircase

31

in a tower from which landings opened out. It had a massive hand-rail with a square-topped newel at each landing for the big oil lamps. The second floor had big sombre bedrooms, each with a four-poster, the red one hung with red curtains and tassels, the blue one in the same style. What might not be crouching on the tops of the canopies or under the ample bed flounces? These, of course, often hid chamber pots, but sometimes I was almost too frightened to pull one out. This is still one of my nightmares. Another is that I find one already too full to use. The marble-topped bedside pedestal table was for the same purpose, with two, but I think, when used, we always hid them under the bed until the latter went modern and ceased to have flounces. The curtains were heavy, with tasselled cords, but could not shut out the owl cries at night. The older dressing-tables had draperies over the mirror.

All the family have had a passion for alterations and improve-ments, not quite so expensive at an earlier time and leading, both at Cloan and at Foswell, where Aunt Edith, a Nelson, was an equally keen alterer, to steps up and down between one level and another. I doubt if an architect was ever consulted until Uncle Richard did his major alterations. The local builder—and ourselves—were good enough. Granniema's bedroom, when I was a child, had a window one could climb out of on to alps of slates with lead ridges and gutters. There was a charming small sitting-room off it, the porch room, all windows, with low window seats and an arched fireplace. Later there was a very large addition to the house, above all Uncle Richard's study and bedroom, in fact a whole suite. The study smelled of leather armchairs, the wood of the bookshelves and his cigars. This was not a place where children were encouraged to go. But there were other, friendlier bedrooms too, and little new turrets and a much nicer WC with a different smell.

From Granniema's little porch room she, or for that matter I, kneeling up with my nose against the window, could look down over the gravel drive, the sweep of green lawn, the hollow hedge of double holly with *tropaeolum* growing through it. Beyond were the cultivated fields, oats, turnips, or hay and pasture ley, and beyond that again the ridge of Auchterarder, and away in the distance across

1. Maya and me, Edinburgh 1904

2. *Boy, when he was twelve and a half*

Strathearn the clefted mountains where the sunsets lost themselves. But in those days there were lots and lots of trains on the main line between us and Auchterarder; on northerly winds we could hear them chugging up the incline, trailing splendid smoke, and always stopping at Auchterarder station which is now grass-grown and desolate.

In one of these cornfields I had very early on a curious adventure. Or had I? The reapers had scythed the oats, the binders following them. I was too small to bind but I was sent out to glean for the old ladies in the Poor House. I would manage an armful of oat stalks and stagger over with them. Probably the end result was that they would be given a bag of oatmeal, but I always thought that my sheaf would be threshed separately. Anyhow, I felt very useful. Then I met a brown hare and we went off and kept house (marriage, as I saw it) inside a corn stook with six oat sheaves propped round us. I certainly did not know that the hare is the Celtic symbol of fertility and perhaps this has no connection at all with what I appeared to be doing in the harvest field. But as I remember it I was married young to the hare.

The difficulty about Cloan was that it was full of ghosts and such. Much of my terror was induced by the elders, my brother and the big Foswell cousins. There was only one younger than me, Foswell Archie, and he was protected by Nana, who would have skelped any of the rest of us. My almost-twin cousin Graeme appeared to be immune to the teasing and frightening. Long afterwards he told me that he too had been scared stiff of the gorgonzola which haunted the tower room, but he had been wise enough to keep his mouth shut. The tower room was round, with the closed-in spiral staircase going up the middle so that if one opened the door into apparent dusty emptiness whatever else there might have been was certainly hiding behind the staircase wall. It still is in my dreams, waiting to come out at me.

Aunt Bay, ordinarily so kind, had invented the gorgonzola probably as a joke, not just to frighten us. Years later when we talked over all this and its dire effect on me, she said I was the only Haldane to have this kind of runaway imagination, something which now she loved and respected. But it was a misery then. And indeed can be still, though without it I would have no wings.

The worst thing the boys did was to take the dummy head on which Granniema's caps were made and put it into my bed. I screamed so loud and long that everyone was concerned, including my brother. He certainly hadn't meant it to be like that. I didn't care for the dressmaker's dummy either; if it started sliding towards me on its three legs . . .

The library with the nice-smelling wooden bookshelves all round and the window opening into the garden, was my favourite place. The big desk, where my father wrote, puffing his pipe, had glass paperweights with a picture of a dog's head inside or somewhere abroad. In the days when suitable Sunday reading was thought to be salutary I found not only *The Pilgrim's Progress*, *The Holy War* and *Foxe's Book of Martyrs* (bloodthirsty all of them) but the *Encyclopaedia Britannica*, which enlightened me on certain puzzling phrases in Leviticus. But there was a room immediately above with games in it. Unreasonably, I hated it, because the steep little stairs had a turn one couldn't see round—and *what* might—? But again, someone may have frightened me deliberately. Uncle Richard's study, a delightful room, and the rest of his suite, were out of bounds until much later.

But outside was different. Here were the peacocks which, if skilfully chased, might be induced to drop a feather. We were allowed to pick these up but not to pull them out, and the temptation of those splendid tails was very strong. I made various houses and forts among and under spruce branches but I was never a good climber. One of our ploys was to steal grapes from the greenhouse; one of the big ones sprawled out so as not to put too much weight on the glass and reached in his arm. We retired up the big lime tree into the summer sound of the bees to eat our spoil, not more than one bunch I think. And I usually had to be hauled up by one of the others. If they didn't I was liable to roam round bleating which might have alerted the grown-ups. All our initials are still up there, growing, with the tree, though some of us are dead and all too old to climb and look.

There were beehives in the garden with little beds of bee flowers growing beside them. The sweet strong smell of honey filled that part of the garden which I remember perpetually in warm sun, though no doubt this happened as seldom as it usually does in Scotland. When visitors were walking past being shown round the policies, as one said, another of our ploys was to lob stones over the garden wall at the hives in the hope of irritating the bees into stinging them or at least scaring them into running away. This happened to various distinguished guests and we found it very exhilarating. Was one of them Baden-Powell? I am sure I was pleased if it was, because he kept stopping me to teach me knots, which didn't interest me at the time. When I had to know them because of using them, they became interesting and I was quite quick at them. But not then!

The walled garden at Cloan, about an acre I think, was a kind of Tom Tiddler's ground where we grabbed and hid and dodged the gardeners until such time as we were old enough to be assumed to be responsible members of the family. Meanwhile there were thickets of raspberries, gooseberries and currants, and along the walls dripping purple plums, apples and greengages. Strawberries were more difficult, offering no hiding places. Beyond there were the garden extensions which Aunt Bay had made, with clipped yew hedges, moss roses and the dogs' tombstones. There had been dynasties of large dogs, labradors I think, Bosco, Ben and Tyne, very amiable to small children, allowing us to share their huge wooden kennel with the doorway just large enough to get into, and even to let us eat titbits out of their bowls. Grown-ups were much less pleasant about this, unkindly pulling us out of the big kennel and talking about fleas.

Granniema had various little cairns, intelligent and not always friendly; they liked to lie on the black hearth rug in front of the shining steel of the drawing-room fire. So did I. The big, chilly drawing-room smelt of dogs and potpourri and the great jars of garden flowers which Aunt Bay enjoyed arranging. This was always done in a little pantry in the passage close to the telephone (the kind with a handle one wound) and the gentleman's lavatory. Any large house would have a WC near the door strictly for the men. If one dashed in because one was in a desperate hurry one felt a deep sense of social guilt. It was still worse, if the hurry was such—as I remember once rushing back from school to the Oxford house with a bladder scarcely in control—that one used the servants' WC. That was almost beyond forgiveness. One only hoped not to have been observed.

There were of course masses of shrubberies at Cloan, nothing like the modern shrub garden with special beautiful flowering bushes, but thick and shiny with dark leaves, laurel and rhododendron meant as barriers and excellent for hide-and-seek. Among these were drying greens, small lawns, and a round pond with a fountain in the middle jetting out from a rockery of stones and ferns which, again, if one managed to turn it full on suddenly might on a favourable wind shower a distinguished visitor. There was also the croquet lawn where we had large mixed games of croquet at which I was very seldom chosen as a partner since I was normally very bad, especially if someone stood over me telling me exactly what to do. But this was in general safe ground where the enemy was not supernatural but only the gardeners and then only if one had been in some way naughty. From the garden an upper and lower walk followed the glen, with the burn at the bottom and at the far side steep fields running up to Foswell; here there were dark bits which I didn't like so much. My father was constantly constructing new walks and Boy was allowed to help but not on the whole a small girl, though I helped to knock down nettles with a stick and called myself 'Nou the Nettle-killer'. There was a time when the walk right along the glen was very tiring and one had to be carried piggyback, one's fat legs rubbing against tweed shoulders. Then in how few years one was carrying one's own small ones.

But once Graeme and I ran all the way. It was like this. There was a house party and Margot Asquith was much taken or pretended to be with Graeme and me. She patted our heads, which we didn't like, and then gave us each sixpence, upon which we turned and ran right up the glen, thinking of all the things we could buy—for sixpence was something in those days. But when we were finally out of breath I had lost my sixpence and Graeme wouldn't share his with me. But I don't mind now!

I never liked having my head patted. When I was taken visiting to the Poor House the old ladies used to stroke my hair. Their hands smelt dreadful, so did everything about them. But as soon as I could read properly I used to be sent down to read 'a chapter from the Book' to one of them who was probably blind. There were various village visits we always had to pay. One sat dangling one's legs on one side of a black-leaded cooking stove trying to be good. Perhaps at the end one got a bit of shortbread.

Apart from social do-gooding there was more of a religious atmosphere up north, though I am sure I never went to church until later on. This was partly because it was a longish walk; we didn't drive on Sundays. I don't think I was brought into family prayers until I was of a comparatively untender age. But then I found them very flavoursome. On a Sunday evening we might be sitting in the drawing-room reading or playing draughts and then came the sound of the big gong in the hall. Hastily one sat up, closing one's book, and the deep purple plush benches were brought in. Then in came the servants in order of precedence, Mrs Cook in some sort of dark satin, the butler, my uncle's chauffeur in a smart suit. He was a Methodist and had adapted the horn of the car to play the first few notes of *Lead Kindly Light* so his appearance at family prayers was an act of courtesy. Then came the rest of the staff down to the youngest kitchen maid. The family of course stayed in their chairs, somewhat cut off by a small table with plants on it. The chairs had chintz covers and white crochet antimacassars, though these were later done away with. There were chintz-covered foot-stools as well, for comfortable kneeling.

The senior male member of the family read the Chapter and improvised a prayer in proper Presbyterian style. When it was my father's turn he refused to improvise but read a prayer in such a surprised voice that it sounded improvised. My brother once produced a very Etonian one, even with bits of Latin in it. I always longed to do it but it was never my turn.

Everyone sat during the Lesson, stood to sing and knelt to pray.

37

Once much later on one of Granniema's cairns leapt on to a kneeling back and walked all the way down along the line, snuffing at necks and ears. The backs stayed splendidly rigid until the turn of the teenage kitchen maid, who heaved with giggles—as I also did.

At first Granniema had been there in charge. Later she was in bed in the room upstairs but she always chose the hymns which Aunt Bay, no musician, played on the seldom-opened black upright piano. They were sad hymns in minor keys, *Sun of My Soul, As Pants the Hart*. I liked them.

Later, when occasionally I went to church with the others, closed in near the back in the family pew, and as a teenager, constantly and painfully afflicted with the giggles, I didn't care for Presbyterianism. There was nothing attractive about building, decoration or congregation. I never even wanted to put the money I had been equipped with in the massive plates at the door under the chilly gaze of the Elders. It was a nice walk back, but Sunday lunch, unless one could quickly get some cold meat, was boiled sheep's head. It had been singed by the blacksmith in the smiddy furnace and cooked with barley. This is something I am very partial to now, but then I hated it, and Uncle Richard would always poke about in it and offer one an eye. That Haldane teasing! How one suffered from it.

But Oxford was utterly different. My parents were among the first generation of agnostics. They had married with the minimal religious service in the Edinburgh drawing-room of my mother's parents, as Scottish custom approved. My brother and I were unbaptised bairns. But the whole family, believers or not, did believe strongly in freedom of conscience for others. When I had something of a fight with my in-laws not to get married in church myself, Granniema backed me up: 'If you're acting according to your conscience.'

I remember being penned in between the back of the sofa and my reclining mother while she read aloud Montefiore's *Bible for Home Reading* which I found dull. There was so little for instance about the animals in the Ark which were surely the most important; they certainly were in my Ark, especially the tigers with string tails.

38

Noah was in a kind of dull brown dressing-gown clasping a dove. Sometimes we went to Sunday evening services at New College where the power of the low organ notes seemed to shudder everything. But again I found most of it dull and always involving being properly dressed and sitting still. Above all it had nothing to do with the terrors and propitiations which went on elsewhere. Would an evening prayer have stopped nightmares? One just doesn't know. It would have had to be on the same level of consciousness and the two layers might easily have missed.

When I went to school I was aware with some smug pride that I was in some way different. I bawled the hymns with the others, usually the jolly ones, but did not join in the Amen which I felt would have put me in the wrong camp. But I certainly joined in scripture lessons and indeed got several prizes. One of my first poems was in the first person about being the elephant chief and successfully getting my wife into the Ark.

V

The Cold and the Flower

Both Edinburgh and Cloan were always cold. Central heating was still in the distant future (after a period of being disapproved of as unhealthy and unnatural—look at the Ancient Britons!) and double glazing even more so. Nor is it entirely simple to put central heating into solidly stone-built Scottish houses. In thousands and thousands of these houses the under servants carried the full coal scuttles upstairs and the empty ones down to the cellars and often had coal-smudged faces. I think my parents worried a bit about them, but probably not the older generation. It was after all their place. They were fortunate to be in 'good service' with security and respectability and the chance to move up.

At the beginning of the century the unders still only got a few pounds a year, but the wages of the senior servants were beginning to creep up. All of course wore long aprons over stuff dresses, ankle length, and white caps, but an upper, especially a parlourmaid, might have becoming streamers and her afternoon apron at least would be starched and tucked muslin. I think there must have been a butler in the Edinburgh house who probably among other things warmed *The Scotsman*—and *Times?*—for Grandpapa (my mother's father) who was fussy about his health. There must have been one at Cloan for there was certainly a butler's pantry where the silver was cleaned and I seem to remember green baize aprons, though I am much clearer about the head ploughman who came from the Mearns, as indeed most of the best farm servants did. I think perhaps the butler came up from London with Uncle Richard, while Granniema and Aunt Bay only had women servants.

A fishwife from Cockenzie called at Grandpapa's house, 10

Randolph Crescent, once or perhaps twice a week, splendid in her kilted skirt and striped petticoat, the creel of fish on her back. Of course the horse vans from the shops with which we dealt called every day, not yet having been partly replaced by the telephone. With luck one might be there when the orders were handed in and might find oneself in the way of sugared almonds, biscuits, cookies or French bread. One after another, the 'good' Edinburgh shops disappear and the supermarkets take over now. It isn't even easy to buy really fresh fish. But in those days people rarely ate out; today's coffee houses and cheerful students make up for a lot.

10 Randolph Crescent towered five storeys up in front, but, as it was built on the edge of a cliff above the Water of Leith, dropped down for countless storeys on the west side, past all of which one must climb to get to the gardens; this was a distinctly alarming process which just appears in my six-year-old diary: 'I went down to the cellars where I saw some things that looked like ghosts. The cellars are covered with Stalagtites; under them are stalagmites which are like bumps of India rubber on the floor. Stalagtites are long thin dark black things caused by water with lime in it driping between the stones in the roof.' Thus scientific interest is allowed to mask the terror. Jack describes it in greater detail with a plan and mention of an old well and pipe which I have forgotten. All this was below the kitchens and the wine cellar, far below Grandpapa's study where gentlemen were allowed to smoke, the diningroom, and above it the great double drawing-room and 'boudoir' where there was a singularly horrid picture on an easel of Boy looking good with long ringlets and a hockey stick. The Edinburgh drawing-room must have been beautiful; there was the long, glassfronted bookcase topped with china, the very best of it in the centre cupboard, pictures, flowers, the gorgeous Worcester tea set and electric light. But, somehow or another, the bulbs done were up in yellow silk bags. Why didn't they get burned? Perhaps they did.

Above them again were the best bedrooms, and the narrower stairs to our rooms above. All has been remodelled inside into unrecognisability. Only the wonderful view remains, north to the pools of the Water of Leith between the high green branches, or down river, and the splendid granite cliffs of the rest of the New Town.

But could Edinburgh in winter have been quite as cold as I remember it outside? Perhaps our clothes were inadequate, though I had a muff on a string and of course gaiters with a row of horrible pinching buttons. Most ladies had muffs and fur necklets for winter, often with an animal's head on one end; these replaced the summer 'boas' of short ostrich feathers, white or dyed, but these were garden-party wear and of little practical merit. Next to us we all wore woollen combinations, thick in winter, thinner and short-sleeved in summer. One had clean ones on Sundays. The difficulty was that the edges round the slit at the bottom tended to get a bit sticky and scratchy. Over these one wore serge knickers, buttoning below the knee, but these had linings which could be changed more often. Men and boys had thick woollen vests and long pants in an unattractive 'natural wool' colour. Combinations went on during all my young life until the early twenties when I cast them off in favour of longish chemises of fine linen or printed silk—and of course I mean real silk—man-made fibres were still rather nasty. But I expect my mother's generation stuck to their ladies' com-binations until the end.

Anyway, that should have kept me warm in the east wind of Edinburgh but I didn't. I was taken for walks, my hand held firmly, but I was allowed to run in Prince's Street Gardens or in the Randolph Crescent gardens that sloped steeply to the Water of Leith and St Bernard's Well, repaired by one of my forbears but whose water I was wisely not allowed to drink. I often hoped I would see a would-be suicide floating down from the Dean Bridge, parachuted by a petticoat as the story had it. Edinburgh pavements were particularly appropriate for the lines and squares ritual with their huge granite sets. I avoided the lines as, presumably, most right-thinking people do. Yet there must be some who actually step on the lines. It would be interesting to know with what other abnormality this is correlated.

I think we must usually have spent Christmas at Randolph Crescent until such time as Grandpapa died and Granny moved down to Oxford, when I was turned out of the nursery to an upstairs room, but at least then we had our Christmas tree at home. Still, Christmas was good wherever it was. How long the grey Edinburgh light took to seep through until one could see the shape of one's stocking at the foot of the bed. Was it as big as last time? Bigger? That promising bulge? Boy and I had separately helped to fill one another's stockings but had kept firm secrets. Some of the presents were wrapped, anyhow. I can't think I ever believed in Father Christmas coming down the chimney, but I gave the notion lip service to please my elders as my own children have kindly done for me.

There wasn't nearly such a variety of toys and games in the shops, though of course there was a blissful penny drawer in the arcade where I sometimes went: this had divisions each holding different penny toys: small wooden dolls or animals, tops, marbles, puzzles, single lead soldiers. That was the best place of all when it came to shops. But in Prince's Street, which must have been then partly unspoiled, there was Maule's at the corner by Charlotte Square, where Binns is now, which had 'ballies', round shells into which one's bill and money were put to whizz up on to an overhead rail along which they trundled to a central desk and then back. How deplorable if two purchases were made at the same counter so that both went into one 'ballie'! Jenner's, however, had a lift. Duncan and Flockart had blackcurrant jujubes which made a cold into a treat and there was also the hairdresser where my mother, before her time with short hair which indeed became her well, had it brushed with a rotary machine. I would have thought it would have been very bad for the hair but she kept hers much the same well into her nineties.

These were lovely shops in a way but, apart from the penny drawer, not for their contents. For that there was only one shop, Liberty's in London. They had the Morris materials and the 'modern' hand-made jewellery. I suppose they had the Morris feeling for crafts and, as I remember, the shop assistants wore real dresses and were considered to be 'ladies' in my mother's sense. One of the few things on which my parents agreed, though possibly for different reasons, was their admiration for Morris and de Morgan. We had Morris wallpapers in St Margaret's Road and the downstairs curtains were certainly Morris materials. I think it was the honeysuckle pattern wallpaper in the drawing-room and a dark red version of the palm tree in the dining-room. And of course the hoopoe was a de Morgan tile. And still is. We had a leadless glaze pottery breakfast set in cheerful peasant colours; at that time lead poisoning was a great hazard in the potteries, so my parents made a willing contribution to industrial health. It was also much better designed than most domestic china of the period—was it perhaps by a Morris follower?

Liberty's had all these materials and some of them were so beautiful, *crêpe de chine* and many kinds of silk and velvet. We went there once or twice a year. My best dress was always a Liberty. There was a long magic passage underground with lighted showcases full of beauty. Many years after, in 1953, I had the same feeling of beauty-shock from showcases at the Britain Can Make It exhibition at the Victoria and Albert after the years of making do with rationing and utility goods. When I was around eleven I spent much time with the illustrated Liberty catalogues—few shops went in for colour-printed catalogues in those days. I had invented a family and I chose them presents, allowing myself one in four of the things illustrated. But it was difficult to find presents for the boys. Could a boy possibly want one of those scarves? Would he ever be able to wear it? Wouldn't it be 'cissy'? Of course no gentleman would ever have dreamed of wearing a coloured shirt. Linen must be seen to be clean—and white. It seems extraordinary that men allowed themselves to be bullied for a whole century by the dullest and most uncomfortable of fashions. No wonder they have broken out since.

At least in Edinburgh one still saw the occasional kilt, though mostly on soldiers. Oh, the glory of the pipers leading the march across the Dean Bridge! One rushed out on to the dining-room balcony to see them. The parapet of the Dean Bridge was low enough for one to be able to see the marchers; it has, sadly, been raised since, I suppose because of those suicides—which must have been rare. Sometimes there were Edinburgh fancy dress parties which I loved above everything. Once I went as Little Boy Blue, actually in boy's clothes, but somewhat rationed on how often I might blow up my horn. Boy wore Indian clothes and I think he had a Sikh turban tied by one of the old soldiers who frequented the house, officers in Indian regiments, cousins or from some equally namely family. I helped to put the brown on to his face and hands. These parties would be at the big houses of friends or fairly remote cousins in the New Town but I remember no childhood mates. Boy was enough for me, and, later, my school friends.

There were, of course, the cousins from Foswell, the Fossils we called them, and a series of feuds and alliances with and around them. Other cousins appeared briefly, Nancy from America and several families from New Zealand, nephews and nieces of our dear Rob Makgill, my father's pupil and our playmate, later Medical Officer of Auckland. I was devoted to several of my father's pupils and young colleagues, especially Teddy Boycott.* And they clearly were very nice to me. It was a satisfactory relationship without too much emotion; that was what was exhausting about parents and perhaps can't avoid being. One has so many feelings of guilt and responsibility which make for emotional tensions.

In my time the earlier generation was rather unapproachable. There were various great aunts or perhaps step-great aunts on my father's side, fat Aunt Eliza and thin Aunt Eliza, one of whom gave me some tiny-tiny bright-coloured wooden soldiers. It must have been fat Aunt, Granniema's sister, because I remember sitting on her knee and arranging them along the great ledge of her bosom where also reposed a gold watch on a brooch and various chains. My mother had two uncles, Uncle Philip and Uncle Jim, with whom she feuded, especially after her father's death, when, so she said, one of them—but I can't now remember which was the baddie—had unfairly got away with some pictures or silver which should by rights have been hers. She was very property-conscious.

* He comes into the diaries. 1904: 'It was Mr. Boycott's wedding day & we all drank his health in champaine at dinner.' 1906: 'Mr. Boycott came to tea, we are always very glad to see him. He has got a baby who he showed us the photograph of.'

As I grew up I became much nearer Granniema, who had I think always been interested in me as a potential artist of some kind. She herself did oil paintings, mostly copies of older family pictures. I have one of her 'Raeburns'; it has considerable merit and feeling and one wonders what she might have achieved if the climate of the times had been propitious.

As soon as I could write at all fluently she got me to write to her, especially with descriptions of wild flowers. Then she would explain how I might describe them better. I became more and more ambitious, keen to observe small matters of colour and texture and habitat. The nearer the ground one is the more fun one gets out of small flowers. Under the bracken near the high summerhouse there was soft grass and in it wild pansies, no two quite alike if one looked close enough. There was eyebright and speedwell, blue harebells and sometimes a white one, tiny shining toadstools, scarlet or yellow, and a kingdom of different mosses. Crawling through, there were dark and light patches, smells of sheep and foxes and the lovely earth itself. By the time I was ten I had my own Bentham and Hooker and was on my way to becoming a reasonably good field botanist.

There were two Cloan summerhouses. One went along the terrace walk to get to them, past gnarled wind-blown laburnums and high cedars and larches, and so to the lower plantation, the zig-zag path up among ferns and foxgloves and the low summerhouse built in a rustic style, heather-thatched and much adorned with Auchterarder initials, though not with the *graffiti* one might expect now. It was somewhat overshadowed by the spruces and could be a little alarming. When I dream of it now I cannot be totally sure that something unpleasant may not happen. But one took the path on and up, along a short stretch of dyke and a small pool for the sheep to drink at, which was interestingly populated by moochs. The high summerhouse was in the same style but less overshadowed and with a superb view north-west across the Strath and the other way to the grass hills that backed us. I think most of the big houses must have had this kind of thing, an object for a walk, kept up by the estate workers. Twice in my lifetime the spruce plantations have been cut and replanted. Uncle Willie from Foswell looked after the estates and made some plantations himself quite high on the slopes of the Ochills. The neighbours laughed about this, saying they would never do and in the early years of the Forestry Commission such planting was unheard of. But he was fully justified even before his death when these grand shelter belts made all the difference to the hill cattle.

Today the terrace walk has changed little, though only one laburnum still stretches a single flowering arm from a much aged and doctored trunk and the great larch boles are so grown that they have pushed the path to one side. The diesel trains sound less alive than the old trains and none stop at Auchterarder station. Both summerhouses have gone.

There were other good walks. I can just remember Auchterarder as it used to be, with an open drain flowing down the street and the stone slabs of the bridges over it from the house doors. Then came the sewage plant with the big septic tank, to which we made an expedition on September 7th 1906; it rates a page of the diary with 'bacteria' properly spelled. But Jack was much more scientific and had several pages and some discussion of typhoid. Later the same day he and I walked daringly through the tunnel under the railway line, which the burn still flows through; how far it seemed to the arch of daylight when one was in the middle!

Once at least in the summer holidays there would be the Craig Rossie walk, though at first I had to be pulled or occasionally carried.* But before one got to Craig Rossie there was the Black Swelch where the Perna burn, swelled by the Coul burn, falls over a precipice into a dark and frightening pool, deep down with only a narrow slippery path to cling to and slip along. Once there was a dead sheep, white and shapeless, swirling in it, but I had a feeling that it might be the kelpie. Miss Delf, who was the 'companion' of Aunt Eliza (which one?), had the then very unusual accomplishment of diving and swimming. She dived into the Black Swelch

* Jack's 1902 diary says: 'This was Naomi's first at all high climb (over 1300 feet high) so we had to carry her and haul her a lot of the way.' But not bad for a five-year-old.

and measured the depth, a thing I can't imagine myself daring to do.

The first electricity at Cloan came from a turbine worked from the dam a mile or so up the burn. This was when Uncle Richard enlarged the house in 1904. Here was another exciting bit of estate work which visitors, taken round the policies, must not miss. The 1904 diary is full of the thrills of concrete-pouring, though this was less exciting than storming wasps' bikes 'so that they got very angry'. In time the turbine also worked the Cloan sawmill but there were constant problems about how much electricity was being used and difficult moments when the engine raced and the lights glared or dimmed. But in summer the dam sometimes held up the flow below so that there was only a trickle of water, and I minded this because I spent an immense time making dams of my own. Here again it was the closeness that mattered; the matching of surfaces, the swirls that pointed the water's diverted way, the moss, the caddis worm casts, the sailing feather, the dappling of light, the cool live push of the burn against one's groping hands. If I ever found a really suitable rock I would make a fairy's garden, busily adorning it until no sensible fairy could possibly pass it by. Of course one didn't believe in fairies but the pleasure of adornment must have some practical basis.

There was busy house-building as well.* Once someone—Miss Delf?—gave me a real china bell that tinkled, to hang outside my current house. But I had a funny feeling that people in the exploring books did it better.

Sometimes we went high up, perhaps to Ramsay's Loup where a sheep stealer was said to have jumped the burn, cliff to cliff. Here there was bog myrtle, bog asphodel, sundew and pinguicula with the marvellous scent of its violet flowers, and grass of Parnassus, perhaps the most beautiful of all the Scottish wild flowers. But the burn itself was too deep and strong for damming until one got much higher up, beyond a child's walking distance.

* Jack's 1902 diary says: 'Naomi and I are building a house of branches round a tree, and thatching it with hay and leaves.'

3. Uncle Richard as I remember him

4. My father as a young man

5. Rob Makgill, our New Zealand cousin, with Boy and me in the garden of the house in St Margaret's Road

6. Granniema at Cloan

VI

Towards School

Once I began to read I gobbled books. One of my favourite reading places at Oxford was the window-seat behind the corner folds of the Morris curtain in the drawing-room. This was also very nice in the evening when the curtains were completely drawn and one could crawl along with the dark garden behind the window panes— for some reason that didn't frighten me at all—and peep through the folds at the lighted room. So much nicer than actually being in it! Like most intelligent children I was omnivorous, and when there was nothing else I tackled books which were much too old for me, including for instance *Dangerous Trades* with its fascinating engravings—not yet photographs—of the ravages of lead poisoning or glass blowers' collapsed chests. I even read the more lurid bits of the BMJ, as well as anything about mine accidents. These were familiar because every time there was a bad mine disaster—and there were a good many in the first decade of the century—my father would take his mine clothes and miner's helmet with the safety lamp and go off to investigate the pit. If after a time we got back a series of telegrams saying 'I am all right', we would know he had got a bad dose of carbon monoxide poisoning which had blotted out the memory of the first telegram. Periodically we would have visits from mine managers and deputies and my mother, who was not too partial to the working classes, welcomed them and fed them. They were—different. So to some extent were others dealing with basic materials, farmers and fishermen.

But to be 'in trade' was the lowest thing, whether you were a shop assistant or a successful contractor—and one or two of these latter shockingly now had sons at the Dragon School which used to

49

be reserved for University children, and also of course whatever parents in the recognised professions, the army, the navy, the church and the bar, might have been found at Oxford. However, University teaching, which was quite badly paid at that time, was not really a thing where one could be certain of finding gentlefolk, though heads of colleges were usually, but not always, acceptable. Their wives were often far from being the people my mother would have considered her social equals in Scotland.

I remember being severely lectured about trade when I was discovered to have made friends behind the counter at the small draper's in North Parade. There were little drawers with buttons and hooks and silk or cotton thread which I had been allowed to look into delightedly and touch, better than a doll's house. I was made to feel naughty, but worst was having to pretend not to be friends with the ladies in the black stuff dresses, to be made to feel they were somehow different, that they 'smelled'.

This trade dislike swept on to include not only managers but directors of large companies. Yet how did this square with early twentieth-century imperialism which my mother believed in so strongly? Joe Chamberlain, her hero? And if she had ever met Rhodes in person? I suppose she managed to surround them with 'the white man's burden' story which she herself took seriously and brought us up on. Which of us don't romanticise otherwise brutal and nasty political realities? But the devoted Briton in an Indian regiment or the ICS or even Africa was the ideal. Her favourite young cousin was actually killed on the North West Frontier and I missed my first ball in Edinburgh. I hardly knew him myself, but had gallons of sympathetic grief for my mother and swallowed my own feelings about the ball. Probably I wouldn't have been allowed to stay late anyhow! I was only sixteen and not properly 'out'. But all this comes very fascinatingly into her own book, *Friends and Kindred*.

My mixed literary diet was reasonably uncensored. It was later on that I was forbidden to read various books, including the works of Anatole France and also *Madame Bovary*. Reading these (as I inevitably did) improved my French but was otherwise disappointing. I did however progress to Balzac's *Contes Drôlatiques*, not forbidden because not known about. Balzac, after all, was supposed to be a respectable writer and there was a complete edition bound in blue leather at Queen Anne's Gate where Uncle Richard had his town house. I do remember that I was considerably shocked by some of the stories, though I was sufficiently curious to go on struggling with their odd French, but they struck me as dreadfully anti-feminist and certainly put me off sex for some time.

But as a child what shocked was entirely different. For instance, I couldn't bear to look at the picture of Alice with the long neck in *Alice in Wonderland* and managed to turn the page quickly so that she couldn't get out. I devoured all the nature books, London and Seton Thompson, and wept over the deaths of Waab (I could still quote that) and the various other animals. If there were children's comics then they were strictly kept away, but I doubt if they had gone far down the age groups yet; rather later I had a Tintin-type picture-book: *Buster Brown and his dog Tige*; I was fascinated by the Americanisms in it. There was *Struwelpeter* which didn't stop me sucking my forefinger—nor did aloes for that matter. There were the *Jungle Books* in which I liked the verse best, and *Peter Rabbit*, though I don't remember any of the other Beatrix Potter books. There was *Little Black Sambo* whom I was delighted to re-meet more than half a century later as a hero figure in a Botswana nursery school. And there were *Flower Fairies*—how I loved those somewhat sentimental pictures! There were other and more genuine fairies in the Jacobs collections with the notes which of course I read. These fairy tales were first read aloud but not *Binnorie* or *Mr Fox*, which it was thought might frighten me. When I read them for myself later they didn't. That wasn't the kind of thing—! Do parents always guess wrong?

I never much cared for the more romantic series of fairytales edited by Andrew Lang in spite of their lovely pictures. Later on when I was eleven or twelve I told him I hadn't liked them and he didn't mind at all; these collections had just been a job. But he liked it enormously when I told him how much I treasured his poems and even quoted some of them to him. Hardly anyone had said anything nice to him about them (and they certainly were minor verse though at the time they rang my bell) but they were, so to speak, his favourite children.

Then there were the first Saga books and *Heroes of Asgard*, as well as a certain amount of perhaps inaccurate anthropology. But there was nothing like the variety of good illustrated popular science and history that there is now. There was also the reading aloud. My mother—Maya to both Boy and me—used to read almost every evening after tea and in this way we went through *The Idylls of the King* and much more Tennyson. I think she must have read very well and I enjoyed it enormously, but prose never quite so much, except for *The Water Babies* where some parts, for instance the descent from the moors into Vendale, are such magnificent Victorian purple patches that they are as memorable as verse. But here the moralities worried me, as in many other books, including most of George MacDonald, though I could treat the early or mid-Victorian moral tales for children with a remarkable degree of contempt and historical interest.

Much of this reading aloud was done while my mother was 'lying down'. I came to accept it as ordinary that ladies did a lot of lying down. That was what sofas were for. Presumably this was part of the routine of menstruation but of this I had no idea. All was completely hidden. I have a notion that at some point my mother had an early miscarriage. All I knew about birth control was that there was such a thing as the Malthusian capsule, pre-sumably an early form of pessary. But this was only hinted at when, shortly before my marriage, my poor mother tried to tell me the facts of life. However, I was determined not to listen. I thought because I had kept guinea pigs for many years and understood Mendelian genetics as far as it had then gone, that I already knew everything.

Reading aloud must have gone right out. I read aloud to my children, and younger grandchildren still like being read aloud to when they are in bed. But I doubt if any right-minded modern child wants to be read to during TV time. Much of my own reading would certainly not have happened if there had been TV or for that

52

matter radio. Even a gramophone was still something quite unusual; we never had one. Newspapers tended to be dull and without pictures, so we never had the awareness of the outside world which a modern child who uses newsprint and TV or radio intelligently would have. We were thrown back much more onto the area of our own imagination, which may or may not be a good thing.

At school we early got on to Macaulay, *The Revenge* and *Lays of Ancient Rome*. How idiotic that one remembers masses of this when things that would be valuable to remember are totally not there. And it is not as if Lordly Volaterrae or even the Forty Prophets were in any way relevant to my life! The multiplication tables should have been drummed in; I had them early. Twice was too easy for colours, but three times was yellow, four orange, five blue. After that they were sombre dark forest tones in which one was lost. Until ten again became clear. But why did I never learn them properly?

Dates elude me still though I am reasonably good on historical sequence and if I am working on a particular period I can manage. But I know where to look things up. That only comes with practice.

I was taught writing in a copy book with 'pot hooks and hangers', the clerkly curves which used thin or thick ink lines which one had to follow. This progressed to copying whole sentences right down a page. But it was dreadfully boring and curiously ink-spreading. One started with a broad-nibbed pen; a fine one would be for later. Fountain pens, still more biros, were very far away. Capital letters might be plain but in the diaries I still tend to make an ornate 'I', 'E' and 'T'.

I found the work in Form 1 of the Dragon School remarkably easy and pleasant and I loved our teacher, Miss Williams, who was small and bright and dark-haired. So I think did everyone else in the class, but how to express it? We were being taught about measures; to make it more fun we were told to guess how big various things were. 'How tall am I?' Miss Williams asked, and I answered 'Eight feet'. Of course I knew perfectly well that she wasn't eight feet, but surely she must want to be and it would give her pleasure if I told her that that was what she was! Alas, no, she was rather cross and told me I was stupid. And how could I explain that it was meant as a compliment?

I think we started Latin almost at once but for a year or two never got beyond the first declension which we all forgot during the holidays, though the early diaries constantly mention 'Doing Latin with Boy'. How long it seemed between one holiday and the next, and endless time till Christmas. One's birthday would never come round again!

The birthday parties were something to look forward to. I was All Saints, Boy was Guy Fawkes. Five years between us, but I liked his friends better than my own age group. We always had a bran pie; for weeks beforehand Maya and I tore up every scrap of coloured paper we could lay hands on and put it into bags until there was enough to fill a tin bath. Then the presents, well wrapped, were put in and a strong cover—oh, the blissful smell of that un-bleached calico—only to be cut open on the day. There was usually another bath where we ducked for apples, since it was also around Hallowe'en time, and I suppose fireworks in the garden for Guy Fawkes. These were lovely and non-lethal compared with today's. I loved holding them and only remember once being slightly scorched. But the main thing was the bran pie and the paper fight that followed, with Maya trying to keep it to one room with the door shut! That made even the tedious hair-brushing I had to put up with afterwards entirely worthwhile. Pleasantly reminding scraps of confettied paper could be found for weeks afterwards in corners and behind cushions.

I suppose we played games like general post, hunt-the-slipper, hide-and-seek, and almost always some of the singing and pulling games, Oranges and Lemons or Nuts in May. It wasn't till much later on at Carradale that I met Dusty Bluebells, Buy Me a Milk Cart, or the Farmer's in his Den. After we moved to Cherwell we started off with an hour or so of out-of-door hide-and-seek with long cross-field chases and dodgings. Tea was always memorable with birthday cake and jellies, crackers and candles. But it wasn't as much fun when Boy was away at Eton. His first year at Oxford he brought friends, including an Etonian friend, Mitch, who had been

Captain of Oppidans and who fell in love with his young sister. But that was far ahead.

For a long time it was mostly one's school friends. School absorbed us. After a term or two, or maybe a year at school, we were told that we were going to learn English grammar. I can't imagine what the mental process was, but it came to me very clearly that this would be in some way damaging and I was not going to touch it. I was quite right in a way; formal grammar would certainly have harmed me as a writer but I had not consciously known I was a writer at that time, nor would the amount of grammar we were likely to learn have been either here or there. A glance at the early diaries shows that I was in little need of it and had a very wide vocabulary. But I refused to learn any of it, which must have been annoying for my dear Miss Williams. However, I did well on the other bits, including as I have said, scripture.

I liked the smell of school, I liked hanging up my coat with the rest. Most of my time I was either the only girl at a boys' school or the only but one, and the other either much older or much younger. But I didn't know or understand other girls—I felt I was a boy who unfairly was not allowed to play rugger (and had no wish to play cricket). The only wretched thing was that when I started school I had also to start wearing black stockings which went right up under my button-below-the-knee knickers. How did they stay up? I think I must have had what was called a liberty bodice with long suspenders attached; I doubt if suspender design has changed very much in half a century. Apart from that I wore a blue serge skirt and a blue jersey, but I did at least have a school blazer with badge. I remember in my first term a boy approaching me with a tin and asking if I would like some bread and cheese. Not being allowed to eat cheese ('It wouldn't agree with you, dear') and supposing myself not to like it, I hesitated. But when he opened the tin it was hawthorn buds which I ate happily and still eat, though they seem rather tasteless now. I felt I was being admitted into the society. It was a nice feeling.

VII

It was True

The Chinnery Haldanes, our cousins at Gleneagles, were all more grown up. We drove over there along the narrow road that skirted the lower slopes of the Ochills with its verges crowded with flowers, the pale Scotch briars and below them banks of wild geranium and St John's wort. One didn't go too far with the carriage horses but one got to know the roads five or ten miles around fairly well. On a hill, any gentleman would get out and walk up, to save the horses; at last I made the point that I could always do this too. Once we got to Gleneagles and had got through the first minutes of polite conversation, there were rooms full of nice things, curiosities or family relics of one kind and another. A family had to have things to show to indoor visitors, just as there were points of interest in the policies for out-of-door ones, and after all, there was always a housemaid to dust them.

The burn was nice, though too tidy for damming; there was St Mungo's well; there was the lime avenue, carpeted in summer with honey-drunk bees; and there was our ruined ancestral castle. It wasn't until I was in my teens that I heard about my back-back-mother, Marjorie Lawson, the Star of Strathearn. My father discovered her in Lindsay and read the poem, which has some remarkably good lines, aloud, somewhat to Aunt Bay's disapproval, since it goes much further than most other poems between then and now. In fact I can't think how this happened: Uffer—my father—was normally rather puritanical in his outlook; I suppose, as Marjorie Lawson was one of the family, whose Haldane husband had been killed at Flodden, it was different. The poem, in fifteenth-century Scots, is probably the first authentic account of a real-life love affair and reads aloud well to this day.

The broken walls of the castle where she played hostess to Squyre Meldrum were fun to climb about and occasionally someone found an ancient bottle, the main thing my ancestors seem to have left. There is also the tiny chapel and graveyard where many of my Haldane forbears are lying or have had their ashes scattered, as my father's were thirty years later, when, after a non-religious cremation in London, organised by my brother and me, the Auchterarder people had gathered to sing *I to the Hills* over his ashes. Aunt Bay and I had been considerably upset when my brother, in the full tide of Communist conversion, refused on principle to have a sleeper and had insisted on taking the ashes up Third Class, in the luggage rack, having ticked me off for being bourgeois, or something of the kind. Irreligious as I am, after that I appreciated *I to the Hills*. The graveyard is in the mouth of Gleneagles with the great slopes of the Ochills, grass and scree and grass again, rising at either side.

Granniema, when it came to her turn, gave instructions for her own funeral: she had reached a hundred and it would have been something of a let-down to live on to a hundred and one. Luckily I guessed that she would like richly coloured flowers and I brought up an armful of red roses and blue iris. The brown farm horses were harnessed to the big red-wheeled lorry with her coffin; all along the ridge of Auchterarder the blinds were down in houses and shops. We and the coffin caught the Edinburgh train at Gleneagles, then Crieff Junction, a special coach I expect, to take us in for the funeral. My father was at that time much involved in a theory about heat engines; also he had somehow got a top hat two sizes too small for him; both these preoccupations kept him reasonably insulated, while I myself was thinking out a poem. I had borrowed a black coat, but it had a blue lining and I needed to clutch this when the time came for all of us descendants to take the cords of the coffin, while the traffic was held up for us across the Lothian Road outside the Caledonian Station.

But that was far ahead. However, we had constant family funerals during my childhood. My mother took the conventions seriously; she was seldom out of half mourning—grey to mauve—

but women did not go much to funerals in those days. My father used to go and clearly found these occasions quite enjoyable. As we say in Scotland, there's nothing beats a good-going funeral.

I did have one heart-tearing experience of the death of a rather older schoolmate; he had played Mercutio in *Romeo and Juliet* and died of pneumonia. Half the school went to his funeral and wept; we kept remembering his lines. I had presumably been a very small attendant on Lady Capulet.

This was how I started Shakespeare. At six I held the train of the French Princess in *Henry V* and, I'm afraid, wetted my drawers with the excitement of the stage. Occasionally this happened at night; one woke up and there it was, warm and wet, and one would be found out. I don't think I was punished but I was certainly filled with shame. I wore white flannel pyjamas with a buttoned flap behind; I did so want proper boys' pyjamas! My dressing-gowns were thick and grey, inherited from cousins, and I didn't much like them either.

There was always one term which, as soon as one got at all far up in the school, was coloured with Shakespeare. I was never worried by the difficult words; they were swept along in the torrent. It certainly made all the difference seeing and hearing it on stage, even without much illusion, after seeing one's brother and his friends making wooden swords and shields. Only the principal characters had proper stage swords and they didn't cut, as everyone soon found out. My mother didn't like the idea of my wearing hired clothes—germs or moral contagion?—so I was often inappropriately dressed. Later, in my last preparatory school year, as Portia, I was lent a Doctor of Science gown from a small physiologist. I had so much wanted to act Lady Macbeth, but I was too short and round and probably not a good enough actor.

At this point a dreadful thing happened. The Prince of Morocco in the casket scene was a boy with a brown skin—was he Indian or perhaps from the Middle East? My mother objected to the mere notion of a mixed marriage and complained to the school. I don't remember what happened, only that it was one more of those social rules which were invisible until one tripped over them, although

58

there was always the assumption that there were things which a lady, however young, should somehow know by instinct. I could understand, when I aided and abetted some gang which was attacking my brother, that I had committed the worst kind of treachery only for the fun of seeing a fight; but these other rules and expectations of one certain kind of conduct rather than another, were very puzzling and became more so as I grew up into a teenager or, as the word was then, a flapper. This referred of course to our hair which was long and worn down our backs, usually with a large bow, and no doubt flapped. Putting one's hair up was the rite of passage to adulthood and a very difficult and boring process it was for ham-handed ones like myself; we were not encouraged to think that it might make one look more attractive or that it would give one any more privileges. Rather the opposite: yet another and stricter code of behaviour.

I find a photograph of myself as Portia. There appears to be no attempt to make me look Elizabethan, though the other actors would have tried their best. Jimmy de la Hey was worried about his very non-Semitic nose as Shylock, but I think he managed to achieve a beard. But I am just a nice little girl in fancy dress. However, I always looked avidly for the review in the *Draconian* and usually felt they hadn't done me justice. We were all very sympathetic with Shylock; I think I was particularly pro-Jewish because of my godfather, Professor Alexander of Manchester who looked like the very best kind of Old Testament prophet. I called him godfather because this was our relationship, but in strict fact he was a Jew and I an unbaptised bairn. We grew increasingly fond of one another; later on I told him about the people I was in love with, and as he never remembered their unimportant names, it was quite all right when I switched.

But this was far on from Portia and the quality of mercy. I learnt by heart easily and now have that bit of my memory choked like a rubbish dump with anything from Shakespeare to Yipiaddy. How grown-up, how sophisticated one felt when bawling those very innocent music-hall songs! But Portia in her long dress—however one seems to have moved around quite easily in skirts

59

which now appear incredibly hampering, especially for the young. In my last year at school we had work squads in our large top English form and the squad leader had to keep up the squad marks in whatever way seemed likely to succeed. I remember chasing two irritating, mark-losing members of my squad round and round the hall with a fencing foil (fencing was thought to be going to make me graceful, but never did). However, whether or not hampered by a knee-length school skirt, I don't think I ever caught them,which was perhaps just as well.

During my time there the Dragon School only staged Shakespeare. Gilbert and Sullivan came later. The arts in general were somewhat marginal and things like drawing and painting taught in such a way as to put one off for life. Shading, right to left—or was it left to right?—on cones or cylinders, no nonsense about drawing out of one's head. No lovely poster colours, only unsatisfactory pale water colours and if we put it on too thick that was wasteful. But of course the margins of all one's school books were copiously decorated, especially the Latin grammar (though I never drew on or knowingly messed up a proper book). It was mostly pen or pencil, though we did sometimes have crayons which melted dramatically when put onto the radiators. All schools must have been a lot messier in the good old days of inkwells in the desks, not to speak of ink-soaked paper pellets used as missiles. Inkwells in desks came in handy. I had a share in a grass snake once (as well as a share in an unsatisfactory dormouse that died before it woke); there was quite a sensation in class when the grass snake put its head out of the ink hole. The desks of course were copiously carved with initials and the soft wood gouged out for railways. Some were good enough to run small marbles along. There is a story which seems well authenticated, though I don't actually remember it, to the effect that my brother and I, in VI B, had both broken silence with the same remark: 'Please, sir, the ink has gone and spilt itself.'

Music was very definitely an 'extra' at school, apart from our thunderous opening hymn. There was never anything in the nature of musical encouragement, nor did I get it at home. But at one time

—I suppose when I was seven or eight—I went to a house further along St Margaret's Road and 'did' piano. Most of it was five finger exercises and very tedious; all that remains for me is the formal ability to read staff, though not to imagine it in my head as sound. In pre-radio days, but after the death of folk music, there was no musical background to living unless specially provided, and this seldom happened in our household, though I think my father whistled in tune, things like 'Robin Adair'. My mother gave me the impression that music and drawing were accomplishments which it was as well to have, but basically a waste of serious time.

I think I had dancing classes as an extra at the Oxford High School in a large hall with windows looking out on Banbury Road. I cannot remember liking them but I did like the school dance which happened once a year, because of the pattern dances: Lancers and Sir Roger, and still more because of the triumphant final rag of the Gallop when one careered down the hall, bumping as many others as possible and quite likely ending in a joyful heap at the far end.

The school classes I remember most clearly were the best and worst taught. The old Skipper, Lynam, our Headmaster, was a marvellous teacher and encourager in all English subjects. He was usually the first recipient of our attempts at 'creative writing'— poems, plays and even essays. He would ask a chosen few to tea with hot buttered toast and anchovy paste, as well as still-warm fudge, and we had what appeared to be immensely intellectual conversation, touching many subjects. Presumably the real thing he did was to treat us as equals, something we didn't get at home. But those tea parties must have been in my last year, at eleven or twelve, when most of the boys were working for Eton and Winchester scholarships, or failing that the lesser 'public' schools, and we had to write Latin verses. This was a bore, apart from the fact that it suddenly came to me that Ovid had shared certain of my experiences: '*Excutior somno, simulacraque noctis adoro.*' Yes, *simulacra*, those were the nightmares, that was the word for them, the things that forced one to fear and worship.

The Skipper was best. The worst was one term or perhaps more of maths teaching which was so bad that it had a lifelong crippling effect. I remember the name and initials of this teacher. He never explained or helped if we really tried to understand but couldn't. He simply taught rules which were as incomprehensible as the social rules which gave me so much trouble. 'Minus times minus is always plus; the reason for this we need not discuss.' Later, from a simple graph I understood in a moment. But the scars stayed.

When I first came, the school was half its present size, with only a few boarders in the house at the bottom of Bardwell Road. This had a lower room where those whose parents ordained such things had glasses of hot milk with skin on them and a Marie biscuit. Oh, how hateful that milk was! Below the school buildings there were wild hawthorn hedges at both sides of the playing fields where we hollowed ourselves out forts and lived the delightful gang life of school children, jabbering away to one another, climbing and tumbling, making up oaths and rhymes. But what was it we talked about? That escapes me entirely, except that it had something to do with status.

There are, however, a couple of references in the diaries to the forts we made in the ditches on the site of the new house. In the 1906 diary, N. Haldane, aged eight, Form 2, says, 'H. Rambaut came to dinner & imediately after that, Jack and Rodney Slessor came and we all went to the site. We found that the ditch was lovely for a fort. Then we put down the rules in Jack Slessor's pocket book, and we decided who was to be chief. I was queen & Rambaut was to be king consort, Jack Slessor was prime minister, Rodney was not anyone particular. After that we broke down the boughs & made at one end a kind of barrier of sticks and stones. Then we had tea & after that we went to where there is a shed & got a broom & we swept out the fort.' After which much time was spent jumping into gravel holes. A few days later Jack Slessor had a party. 'We went to his fort; it looked lovely, with flags hanging on string across it. We then took our weapons—Slessor took an old rusty toy gun, Rambaut took the banner of the fort, De La Hey took a stick, I took a broom & Rodney took another stick. We marched about & then Rodney fetched a dusting sheet & we went to the pavillion of the cricket field . . .' Here the dusting sheet was spread, there were sentries and a 'snoring competition' and after tea we got the weapons and attacked the nursery and made another camp. Later on, at the site, after someone had caught a dragonfly 'I made a law: there shâll be no murder comited in my premises, upon man, nor beast, nor bird, nor fish, nor insect.'

In my last years at school there was much building and enlarging and cutting of the wild hedges and climbing trees with the well-worn hand holes and interesting fallen logs. But I suppose the main hall remains much as it was, though no doubt without the racks of dumbbells and Indian clubs which we used for drill—Indian clubs were great fun to swing, though sometimes we knocked one another on the head with them. 'Sergeant' used to take school drill and taught us some gymnastics, including very enjoyable things like upside-down swinging on the rings.

The western sun streamed into the hall through the large windows at the back of the wooden stage with the piano and the parallel bars standing in front. Here we played our seasonal games, especially in winter when it was cold for playing outside. Conkers gave way to marbles, to whipping tops or sometimes to stilts. But there were always games of He and touch wood going on, with the flee-ers and catchers darting through the rest or jumping over them. Between lessons there was always five minutes of violent play activity allowed, and again at the end of the afternoon. I was bad with tops but fairly good with the various games of marbles and the arguments they gave rise to. Some of the games were simply rolling your marble into little pyramids of the other side's or getting them through bridges cut out of a bit of plank. I got very fond of some of the glassies and there was a terrible thrill in putting them into danger of being captured.

There was one evening in the hall of late golden light and the unmistakable noise of the marbles ringing and rolling on the wood floor, hundreds of them, and the voices of my school mates, all in a state of pleasure and purposeful activity, and I was running round, not even, I think, playing He, just swinging up onto the platform

63

off the parallel bars. I looked down the hall and I thought in a flash, I will remember this all my life. It came to me as certainty on one running foot before the other touched ground, and then I was off again. But it was true.

VIII

Sennen Cove

My father was asked to deal with ankylostomiasis in the Cornish tin mines. He went down to Cornwall and the family followed, looking for a place to stay during the Easter holidays. We got to Penzance and either then or later I went along the causeway to St Michael's Mount and climbed up through more daffodils than I had ever seen. Then from Penzance we started out in a carriage and somehow arrived at Sennen Cove and Mrs Pender looking out of the front window in her stays. At that time the Cove was very much a place on its own with only a few families so that most people were known by their nicknames. Mrs Pender took in a few lodgers and kept the Ship Inn where the fishermen went whenever they had enough money for a glass of beer, which wasn't always. I am quite sure she knew the state of the finances of every family in the village and sent the man home if she knew the wife needed the money more than he did.

Here we went back and back every Easter holidays; I couldn't have borne to go anywhere else. The house had, I think, two small sitting-rooms and the kitchen below and four bedrooms above, one so tiny it just held a bed, no more. If the rooms seemed small to me at five they must indeed have been small; one had to squeeze round the square dining-room table to get into the window bay, or else dive under the table cloth. On the walls there were painted glass rolling pins and the occasional text. There was an earth closet outside; lighting was by lamps. My mother's class prejudices didn't happen at the Cove; these were fishermen and they were different. Mrs Pender spread warmth. I spent a lot of time in the kitchen, helping or hindering her in skimming the Cornish cream from the setting pan on the side of the range or kneading the dough for 'little mansions', small crusty loaves eaten hot with salt butter or cream. When the grey mullet came in we always had mullet baked in milk.

Mullet and pilchards were the money-earners. Watchers from the cliffs and high dunes saw the shoals and signalled to the pair of boats which brought in the two ends of the big seine net; it was all hard rowing. Then every man in the place came down to haul; if it was a big catch it would be all they could do to get it in. At last the bag was in, the fish leaping and dying; they were put into piles as equal as possible, a great circle and a fish left on each pile as the men went round, with half or quarter shares for widows and orphans of fishermen, this being before the days of social insurance. Then everyone, the rowers, the haulers, the watchers, threw some kind of token into a basket, a knotted handkerchief, a root, a piece of seaweed; someone was blindfolded and led round, throwing down a token for every pile. How proud I was when Boy, who had been hauling, got a quarter share! Soon enough I began to feel with the fishermen their hatred and distrust of the middleman, the dealer with his donkey cart who bought their fish and gave them so little for it.

Only a donkey cart, a jingle, could get down to the Cove, slowed on the steepness of the road. That first day we must have left the carriage up at Sennen and walked. Probably I had to be carried up. From that time on, year after year, we went down to Cornwall at Easter and I would know that somewhere in the luggage would be the big cardboard Easter eggs and sometimes Easter presents from other people, including once a cardboard fish full of sweeties with a flap in his side shut by an elastic so that it sounded slock, slock, as one let it spring back: the slock-fish, I kept it for many years. I think we took the night train to the west, for I know once I was sick in the dark. We crossed the bridge from despised Devon to adored Cornwall. I could read the station names: Camborne and now we were near the tin mines where Uffer was working, seeing how his advice was being taken: Dolcoath, West Kitty, Levant, the immensely romantic names of the mines. Then the hill to Gwinnear

Road—have I got the name right?—and the sea, turquoise blue between red cliffs and tunnels, at last Penzance and the drive to Sennen and at once, at once, down to the beach to see if it was altered. There were the two breakwaters of rock and tremendous, squared timbers thick with barnacles, where the Atlantic cable went in, and then a group of great granite rocks with a perpetual spray-fed triangular pool in the middle of one. But how big? Sometimes the sand was washed high round them, sometimes dragged away by the spring tides. But were the rocks five or ten feet high? I suppose they are there still, but how polluted, what would I find? Beyond were other rocks and a series of interlinked rock pools fringed golden brown with seaweed, bottomed with delicate wavering sand patterns. My practised eye looked for dam sites. All that fine sand far along the bay was utterly washed and smoothed, never an oil spot, but along every tide mark an infinity of tiny lovely shells.

Boy had a proper shell collection in a glass-fronted cupboard, his museum; there they were, on cotton wool, in match boxes, labelled with their Latin names. Later on, when I too had a glass-fronted museum, it was full of much more heterogeneous things, though I certainly labelled most of them. There was for instance a stuffed lizard and a kiwi skin, smelling strongly of pepper. Who wants a kiwi skin? I did. And then, later on, suddenly one doesn't.

I collected the shells for their beauty and fragility and especially I loved the small, magic, spotted cowries. Those waves that brought them were the great Atlantic rollers coming strongly, beating themselves out on the sand, so that the air everywhere and especially at high tide was full of a salt luminous mist. The wash and foam of the waves sucked round my ankles and knees; I ran towards them and back; I could not swim, though now, dreaming of Sennen, I often swim or struggle to swim in the great crests and hollows. I was not supposed to get wet through more than once a day, though I can't think why I didn't get wetter, for I wore a school skirt and jersey or a cotton smock to below my knees and usually a hat of some kind, probably a tammy with a toorie on the top where the knitting was held in. Almost everyone wore a hat then. On sunny days my mother wore a straw boater, hatpinned through to a curler in her short hair. For best she had a boater with cherries on it. Boy wore a school cap; my father wore a tweed one and, usually at Sennen, tweed knickerbockers and thick woollen stockings. For years I had a wooden spade, then was promoted to a metal one; immense activity went on all the time. One never walked when one could run. We weren't supposed to play on the rocks in front of the single row of cottages; this was where everything was chucked out and it was probably mucky, though a strong high tide washed everything away. I can't remember the beach or the further rocks ever being dirty, as we know dirt on beaches now.

There was a broken bit on the way down to the beach which was crammed with mesembryanthemums, though we only saw them in flower if we stayed late. But there were sea pinks and scurvy grass with its uncomplicated sweet smell which mixed with the smell of perpetual spray. Behind the beach were long bare sand dunes and marram grass and nobody there. At the far end a small stream edged through the sand and down. Beyond, there was a path up to the cliff tops and along to Genver, the next beach; in later years I followed it on towards the Lizard, again never meeting a soul. On the way there was a small field where someone was growing narcissi for the early London market; there were stone dykes and stiles of upright stones which I was soon big enough to climb by myself. I liked to run along the sheep path at the very edge of the cliff. At this side of Sennen the cliffs were low and climbable; sometimes one had to climb if one had tried to walk round from Genver across the rocks and the tide caught one. But at the Land's End side there were tremendous sheer cliffs and the sea boiling on half-submerged rocks far below.

Here too what I liked best was climbing out onto ledges where I could look down on the heaving, creaming waves. It makes my head swing even to think of it now and Maya clearly showed considerable moral courage in letting me do it. But I wasn't bothered by heights until suddenly in my teens that came on me. I thought I would cure it by walking round the slightly sloping parapet of the laboratory where I was learning as a young Home Student. But when I had made the round I was worse than before. My father didn't like cliff tops and fussed at Boy and me, but luckily was quite without vertigo feelings underground (or in the dark) so that it didn't interfere with his mining activities.

He took Jack to Dolcoath mine and I was very jealous, but probably, at seven or eight, I couldn't have managed the rhythmical stepping on and off a man-engine, the stepped beam going up and down a shaft where the miners clambered in and out of the tin mines.

There is an early letter from my father to Jack, who must have been about ten at the time. He had been down Levant, a very hot mine, and said it had taken three-quarters of an hour to get up or down on the man-engine, being careful to keep to the middle of the step; he ends, 'I think I am going to dream about it all tonight.' They went deep and lost their way in old workings before the mine manager discovered a way out. At that time his temperature was 103. These mines were damp and ill-ventilated, but it appears that they had got to grips with the ankylostomiasis problem, largely through better sanitation. All through the letter, Jack is written to as a fellow scientist.

But there were still a few mines worked from adits, tunnels in the cliff face. Maya and I went into one of them; the red stained water trickled past our feet and the sound of the waves coming in and crashing on the rocks far below the mouth of the adit made a chill, frighteningly enlarged echo.

There were always two or three books for me to read on wet days on holiday and I had to spin them out. Hardbacks of course, and always with pictures. *Captains Courageous* was wonderful to read at Sennen within sound of the sea. So were the Marryats, though the moralising always made me a little uncomfortable. The Nesbits were beginning to come out and one looked forward passionately to the next. There was one at least every two years, but Maya somewhat disapproved of *The Railway Children* where the heroine actually kisses a porter. At this stage I began deliberately identifying, with Alice among the Wouldbegoods and with Anthea in the other family, though I was perhaps more Jane-like. I saw the older boys like my own Boy.

There were holidays tasks for Easter and summer, mostly, apart from the summer diaries, required reading. Certainly *Ivanhoe* and *Quentin Durward*, of which I remember nothing. Some Dickens, probably *A Tale of Two Cities* and *Oliver Twist*. Both these have vanished as well, though I had to pull out *Oliver Twist* again sixty years later in order to help teach it to an English class in Botswana. Here I was struck by its remarkable inapplicability as a school book; in fact I had to spend most of the time telling the class that it was no use learning Dickensian slang to make easier conversation with an Englishman, nor did they have to fear having to eat oysters if they ever came overseas.

At one point—I suppose I was eleven or twelve—Jack tried to get me to read *The Pickwick Papers* which he himself much enjoyed. But I never could like them nor, until many decades later, *Jorrocks*. I think we must have had *Treasure Island* or *Kidnapped* as a holiday task and I never liked them either, though I lapped up plenty more of Stevenson, especially the poetry and the fables and for that matter *Catriona*. Perhaps it was simply that these were set books which put me against them? How universal is that? I see from the diaries that Jack was reading *Gulliver's Travels* aloud to me at five. It might have been his holiday task but I don't think I got much out of it. Isn't it a little hard on Swift to have one bit of his great morality work presented as a children's book?

I read some early Sherlock Holmes but found *The Hound of the Baskervilles* very frightening, and indeed the whole business of fear and capture. I've always been to some extent on the murderer's side so thrillers are not for me. But they had barely started then, though I remember later on a grown-up conversation with Uncle Richard praising *Trent's Last Case*. There was little in the way of what is now called the teenage novel and which in general means a story written straight, in the sense that it has a recognisable beginning, middle and end (which should be fairly happy and conclusive) and without a predominant motive of sex, though the present trendy ones have real-life incidents such as rape, pregnancy, incest and preferably something about racial conflict in which the whites are normally the villains.

This meant that I read a few children's books like *Holiday House*, which had 'morals', as indeed the Nesbits have, though less obviously, and as most books written by socially conscious authors for whatever age group must have. But much was adult, including a lot of exploration books and of course bloodthirsty *Pilgrim's Progress* and *The Holy War*. This led to a lifelong dislike of marmalade since I was taken on a school expedition to Cooper's Oxford marmalade factory and convinced myself that the boiling cauldrons were full of martyrs. Or perhaps I disliked marmalade anyhow and was looking for an excuse not to eat it?

Most years we made an expedition from Sennen to a garden at or beyond St Just where I was told I could pick as many flowers as I wanted; afterwards we sent them off in shoe boxes to friends in Oxford or London; there were fewer flower shops then and better parcel posts. This garden had darkly shining hedges, probably of camellia, and below them daffodils and narcissi so thick that no picking made any difference, hyacinths, early tulips, grape hyacinths, huge umbels of polyanthus primroses, oxlips, and snowflakes, periwinkles; I swung with the bees in the thick scent, close to the texture of the petals. I think we went to other houses, though much later to Eagles' Nest, on my one disconcerting adult visit to Sennen, when I was interested in talking League of Nations politics with Will Arnold-Forster and barely noticed a small boy stalking off into the distance: and coming back from it much, much later, to be my son-in-law.

There were other flowers. Behind Mrs Pender's house a steep path wriggled up the hill towards Sennen Churchtown. There was a great boulder overhanging me and the path, with a trickle of wet through moss and hartstongue fern, and below, under one's delighted eyes, damp silk-smooth violets and furry primroses. The path eased off into a field of daisies, thousands of them and the sweet April smell as one climbed the stone dyke. Near the cliffs there were creeping willows and blue squills and, in the last year or two when I was becoming a passable field botanist, some rarish bog plants.

Most of Cornwall was Methodist, needing a strong religion to tide them over their troubles. (To quote from a sermon, contrasting the welcome for the lax congregation compared with that prepared for the Minister himself: 'Well done, thou good and faithful servant, M. J. Thomas of St Just!') There was a Mission Hall of tarred wood at Sennen. All kept the Sabbath. Once a fisherman with a sick wife, so that money was desperately needed for doctor and medicine, fished on a Sunday and sold his catch. Nobody would speak to him until my father put it to Mrs Pender that he must be forgiven as, for him, it was a work of necessity, and then he and my mother, who also was much liked and respected, went round the Cove, persuading people that he must be taken back. My father did some doctoring himself; these were the days before the Health Service when everything had to be paid for—or begged—and a long illness could cripple a family.

There was little in the way of amusement for the Cove, other than beer: no cinema, no radio. Almost every year we thought up some kind of entertainment, held perhaps in the Mission Hall, which usually centred on our Magic Lantern (also much liked at children's parties at home). This must have worked from an oil burner and magnifying glass. We had coloured slides on which you pulled a lever and changed something, so that a man hammered or shot a tiger, or a dog jumped out of a box; on the nursery rhyme slides there was first Miss Muffet, then (to cheers) the great spider on the next slide. There were also educational slides of foreign countries or British soldiers in acts of gallantry. The show always began with the Flag (a hand-coloured slide of the Union Jack) and ended with the King. And how the audience enjoyed it! Boy and I also thought up tricks like magic writing with lemon juice and there were little presents of striped sweets for the children which I had helped Maya to put into screws of paper folded down. Yet there is a curious contrast with this in Jack's 1903 diary where he goes to 'a kids' party at Strathallon' where there was a cinematograph 'including a coloured film'. Not really a colour film, but perhaps some kind of coloured cartoon? I wonder.

We were down at the harbour often enough, I perhaps carried there by Robbie Pender, blue-eyed and blue-jerseyed, with whom I was in love. I could reach up and just touch his gold ear-rings. The spoken language still used thou and thee; children were childer. It was pleasant on the ear. There were two breakwaters, enclosing arms for the fishing boats; it was exciting to watch them coming home under sail or oars with a gale coming up, hanging back for a wave and then plunging in between the breakwaters on the crest. Once I was taken down at night to see the lifeboat, of which the Cove was so justly proud, launched for a rescue. Every week or fortnight a boat went out to the Longships lighthouse. I was thrown from the tossing boat into arms waiting to catch me on the great rock; there was heaving green water below but nothing to fear. Boy and I showed the lighthouse crew how to feed sea anemones which they had never thought of as living animals, and we explored the lighthouse and the rocks.

Once my mother and I went to the Brizens, the great twin rocks that one saw far out across the bay, the first womenfolk, they said, to land and come off alive, for a ship-wrecked woman had once died there. Every cleft was full of birds' nests, though the species kept well apart. One could stroke the handsome Welsh parrots, the puffins, while they waited on their nests. But the black, snake-necked shags kept strictly to their own part of the rock and jagged with their beaks at anyone who tried to touch them. Cowloe, the skerry just beyond the harbour, was a huge—but how huge was it really?—low-tide island, a whole new area to explore with bigger sea anemones and darting rock fish. One could just wade out through great snaking fronds of kelp, at least Boy did, for one might slip and he could swim.

Some day I supposed I would swim, because in summer I was taken down to the Rhea bathing place in a Cherwell backwater, changed into a musty blue serge bathing dress coming to the elbows and below the knees, with a braided collar which was supposed to hide the figure when one started to have one. I hated being pulled along at the end of a pole and the shallow end was muddy. However I had been promised a canoe of my own, when I could swim, though I don't think I got it till I was eleven or twelve, after my broken leg. By that time I had swum my test (July, 1909) and went

73

swimming whenever and wherever I possibly could, though this was somewhat restricted because the Thames Conservancy in theory did not allow mixed bathing after 8 a.m. However nobody could prevent me falling out of my canoe on a nice sunny afternoon whenever it seemed appropriate.

But not swimming didn't seem to matter at Sennen. Sometimes when my mother and I were sitting out on the cable breakwaters, a wave would break green over our heads and we clung onto the stones. But I was never afraid.

In those days one was always making dares—run round the rocks in the perilous gap between wave and wave, jump, guess, swing, climb! Up to a certain age this goes on. In the thirties Agnes Miller Parker and I swam like porpoises in dangerous waves in the Canaries; I just got back to land out of the sucking surf at Zaraus. But today, at Kovalum, I dodge the crashing breakers, I don't want to get knocked down and hurt. Sadly, one can no longer trust one's nerves and muscles; the balance that made rock-jumping such fun has gone; one becomes less friends with one's body. At last, perhaps, one only remains on terms with certain bits of the brain.

Memory, going back, halts again in 1934, when I went back with my young sons. Mrs Pender was still there then, and so was much of Sennen, though the road had been repaired and there were more visitors' cottages. But the sand was still clean and the great tides only brought in the age-old things of the sea. I wrote this poem then, about Genver.

I am going to find cowries and fan-shells
On a far beach,
Where the sea at half tide breaks, breaks from the clean sands,
Where the spray, blowing and blowing inland, salts the blurred cliff,
Blurring and dumbing the sun-light,
As the continual wide rushing of the waves dumbs
Voices of women or sea-birds.

Do I know danger of quicksands, of the footsteps going one way
   only?
On the cliffs Spring is delayed; the heart checks, daunted.
How then shall flower the stonecrop, how the wind-rocked sea pink?
The cave echoes the wind and waves, will echo tonight
When the rushing purposeless high tide has licked my footsteps out,
Flattening the pale sand for dawn.

But I am finding cowries and fan-shells
On the far beach,
Which is beyond the beaches I know or remember or have imagined.
But the beach will cease to have hold of me and the long pounding
   of the waves
Will beat faintly across damp acres of air, and I shall tread
Stonecrop and cliff turf, with my hands closed upon
Cowries and lovely fan-shells.

IX

Surgery

That broken leg after which I learned to swim was not the first accident in the family. The worst was Boy's fractured skull, when he fell off the step of Uffer's bicycle. If it had killed him my parents would both have been heart-broken, but my mother would always have put the blame onto my father—she had said Boy wasn't to ride on the step, and now— But he survived a fracture of the base of the skull, beginning to ask questions about it the moment he was conscious. Absolute quiet in the home, where he lay in bed in the the spare room, was essential. I understood. For him, I fell all the way down a flight of steps and never squeaked.

I myself had an ordinary concussion, being taken out for a walk with my nurse, tumbling and hitting my head on a road crossing. I was only unconscious for a short time, coming to in a chemist's shop, being given something nasty in a glass. We walked back along Woodstock Road and I began to cry with the pain in my head. The one thing that is clear about this is being scolded by my mother for crying in the street, a thing strictly forbidden in the code of courage. My nurse intervened. I was in bed for several days and found the quality of my life subtly changed from before the unconsciousness, which was in some sense a dream period, to after it which was either now and real or a different dream. This wore off, only return-ing much later, more violently and nastily, when I took mescalin as an experimental guinea pig and felt that the experience had shifted me, so to speak, on base, turning my whole consciousness at an angle to its own past. This took years to wear off completely.

The broken leg was something else again. It must have been in 1905 or 1906 that the Oxford pageant took place; pageants were

76

being held all over England about then, especially in towns with a colourful history. I longed to be in it and was asked for, but it was thought better not. Why? My health, with the TB threat? Or was it that this affair was as much town as gown and I might meet unsuitable people? Instead I was promised a pony, which I didn't much want, though I understood that it was something little girls ought to want.

We were then moving from St Margaret's Road to the large and ugly house, Cherwell, at the bottom of Linton Road. It had fields and hedges, was almost an estate, and was no doubt suitable for riding. But I had to learn to ride side-saddle in a long riding habit. By that time there was a coachman, Crackston, ex-army, rather a brutal man, I think, and not a good teacher.

However, a certain physical toughness was *de rigueur*. My brother was sent to Eton with a broken arm still in a sling and was much teased and tortured by his savage contemporaries for a year and a half. College was a barbarous place and the Master in College had little control over traditional bullying, was probably scared himself. Two seniors for whom Jack fagged, Geoff Wardley and Julian Huxley, saved him to some extent, but he begged to be taken away. When he told me in the next holidays what they had done to him, I tried to get my parents to take his side, but they apparently paid no attention. How could they have taken a son away from Eton and sent him, say, to Radley? The only clue is one letter home, desperately worried because the ten shillings for his fare home had unaccountably disappeared from his 'burry'. Clearly he counted on that leave. He is doing well at school, but 'I am rather sick with people and things in general. Goodbye.'

Certainly he enjoyed Eton later on when he could no longer be bullied, but had made his mark intellectually and quite enjoyed his activities as a wet-bob. But was it something which left permanent scars? I enjoyed Eton too, later on as a visitor, and was once smuggled in and hidden in a cupboard in College during a tremendous battle with Oppidans; the missiles I remember were lump sugar and tin baths. But again, what kind of people is that supposed to produce? I think one knows.

As far as I was concerned, the riding lessons scared me stiff. I was always falling off, never managing to develop the balance or the muscles for side-saddle, and it often hurt a lot, though I didn't cry. I had to go on with them. I don't think Nopy, the pony, was well trained; she was rather an odd creature, with a habit of galloping round and biting off the heads of the ducks. I had a safety stirrup, but in one fall it didn't work. Crackston couldn't catch the pony, which galloped off, dragging and kicking me. I knew I had broken my leg but didn't realise I had also broken one or two ribs and dislocated my neck. It was my tenth birthday.

It was a compound, comminuted fracture of the femur. I dropped out of an entirely new dimension of pain into chloroformed dark, woke immobilised and sick, my head held in place by hard pillows. I was at home, in the big spare room and perhaps safer than at any hospital of that period. One must remember that treatment at home was still usual until at least the middle thirties; my children and husband all had tonsils out at home. One son had an appendix out. The well-scrubbed kitchen table, mackintosh-sheeted, was usual. Nurses would come in, but servants cleared up.

The surgeon came in almost every day, adjusted the weights on my broken leg and tried to help where the cast chafed; his breath smelt of whisky but he often had a small orchid in his buttonhole— he grew them—and would usually give it to me. He had to have a good look at the top of the cast on my femur, but my mother in the curious interests of decency, always hid my very immature sexual parts with a large handkerchief. Perhaps also a surgeon was still considered a social inferior, nearer a barber than a doctor. I don't know what analgesics were in use; I remember none. But perhaps they existed.

An X-ray machine was brought to the house to see what was happening to the broken bone. This must have been fairly early in X-ray development. It took a long, painful time, with the leg being moved and nobody scolding me for crying. Perhaps they X-rayed my neck too. Nobody then thought of screening X-ray operations; the damage was yet to become apparent.

I had a succession of nurses whom I hated, who frightened me in dreams. I fell from one nightmare into another. The leg was re-set under open ether; one struggled against the stinking suffocation. I was extremely sick afterwards, but was given some kind of opium mixture which cured this. Two months went by. At last the weights were taken off; the ribs and dislocation had mended. I was carried down. There was a Christmas tree in the hall and the branches were swung over me with the lovely once-a-year spruce smell so that I could decorate them with tinsel and beautiful birds with spun glass tails.

But in the end the cast was taken off; some of it had stuck and the skin was pulled off too; I still carry the scars. The surgeon tried to bend the knee. It had been immobilised for three months or so and of course was almost a hundred per cent stiff. So I must do exercises, and now I was in the hands of a physiotherapist, Jo Phelps, who bicycled in every day. She must have been very good; in spite of the fact that it hurt like mad, I liked her enormously. But little movement returned. I remember the surgeon saying to my mother: 'This child will never run again', and I made up my mind that whatever I had to stand, this was not going to be my future.

They decided to break the adhesions under an anaesthetic; this time it was nitrous oxide without oxygen, a new kind of suffocation and plunging into a pit of diminishing lights. One struggled and died. Coming to, the knee hurt enormously, but the exercises went better. I was left with an oddly misshapen right patella which, however, gave no trouble for over sixty years, and one leg two inches shorter than the other. They were always measuring them and there was talk of a boot. But I made this difference up on a laterally tilted pelvis which made childbirth slightly more difficult. But for weeks and weeks I went on with the exercises every day, the knee being bent over a table at first, then kneeling or otherwise getting flexure. I could walk. At last I could run. Clearly some bad effects went on. For many years afterwards I was constantly spraining my ankles, both that of the broken leg and of the other, which took the extra strain. These were never bad sprains, but did land me with unpleasantly thick and misshapen ankles.

After the first few days of the accident I read and read, all sorts of books, or else I was read to. I didn't want to slip back at school, nor did I. But I read unexpurgated Grimm which was nightmare stuff and all Hans Andersen, some dreadfully sad, but beautiful. It must have been then that I was first enchanted by Dulac's pictures; I think the Skipper gave me the first of these, probably the Kipling poems. I don't know what happened to them, but I remember the pictures in detail. I also read eagerly the bound volumes of *Aunt Judy's Magazine*, especially the part about the poor little girl in the Aunt Judy cot at the Children's Hospital, with 'hip disease'.

Then they decided to operate on my neck glands, which had got worse with the dislocation and appeared likely to burst. For this I was taken to a London nursing home, which must have been very expensive. I begged not to be given open ether, but of course that was exactly what I was given, and without pre-medication, although at that time and for much later, an enema was standard. The anaesthetising was as unpleasant as ever though I tried not to struggle, but it left me sick for days; this strained the stitches and opened the wounds. I begged for some kind of opium, remembering how it had helped the last time, but did not get it. The surgeon was away for the week-end. I recovered physically with great speed, but it took much longer for the mental effects to wear off. If they ever did.

While I was getting well I did a lot of cutting out pictures for scrap books. This is a form of occupational therapy I still enjoy. At this time the old Edinburgh scrap books lived inside red flannel cases in the middle drawer of the drawing-room bureau. These had some enchanting pictures dating from the period when much trouble was taken with naturalistic detail and any kind of impressionism was still far in the future; there were also genuine scraps, the kind one bought in sheets and separated with scissors, soldiers and children and flowers all in shiny colours. There was much patriotism; there was Bugler Dunne, a young hero of the Boer War. Even with those very unpleasant and somewhat shaming two years in the memory of many, soldiering was still thought of as 'fun' or at least a supreme adventure. But then war at that time was still fairly likely to produce a few heroic situations and emotions among the combatants. Perhaps it helped to have illustrators rather than

7. Cloan

8. *A corner of the drawing-room of 10 Randolph Crescent*

photographers to do the recording. One of my other favourite reads was the bound back numbers of *Punch* with plenty of noble Britannias.

April at Sennen and then I went back to school and had two good years in the upper forms, and watched the new boarding house being put up. The Skipper wanted to take me on one of his Blue Dragon cruises but again I was not allowed. Instead of 'Games' —and I really would have liked playing rugger—I used to go rowing on the Cherwell with Jack Slessor. The river was empty enough for rowing boats in those days; we rather despised punts. He too was out of school games, since he had a lame leg, almost certainly polio, though my mother, typically enough, said his nurse had dropped him and this came of leaving children in the care of servants. I suppose polio, then undiagnosed, was often blamed on someone in this way. Jack and I were very good friends and talked a lot between rowing; I'm sure the British Empire came into it. Both of us read Kipling. Jack desperately wanted to go into the Army, following his father, but this ambition was thought to be hopeless. But his elders and advisers had not reckoned with modern technology, so Jack is now Marshal of the Royal Air Force and covered with medals, all well deserved.

There were other friends, Richards and Rankin—we surnamed one another in those days—Carline (whom we somewhat looked down on because his father was a painter and he wanted to be one) Jack Smyth, later a V.C., and one or two others in our gang. Occasionally we played Devil-in-the-Dark, groaning and flashing lights at passers-by out of hedges, delighted if they ran, and sometimes we were intellectual and devised plays. Mine (like Shakespeare's) were usually in blank verse with a rhyming couplet at the end of each act, but often had difficult stage instructions, like the one about Hannibal in which his brother's head, bleeding, was thrown in for him to soliloquise over. Of course this might have been quite the thing for the Royal Court if it hadn't been two generations too soon.

At one time Jack Slessor and I formed a kind of literary partnership. We wrote a who-dunnit play with revolvers and detectives and carefully designed exits and entrances, which perhaps were a wee bit tricky. It never actually got into production, but involved lots of pleasurable and exciting meetings and conversations. We could be so enviably single-minded about such things, not letting any other aspects of the world interrupt, the way they do now.

I didn't try riding again for some fifty-five years, and then not side-saddle. But I was quite attached to the pony and, later on, used to drive her in a four-wheeled open pony carriage. I often took this down-town into Oxford and either knotted her reins onto a lamp post or gave them to some small boy to hold while I did the shopping. This was a perfectly safe and sensible thing to do pre World War I. In the end, after much wear and tear, the pony carriage came in two in the middle, leaving my governess (for by that time I had left school and was being governessed) in an undignified posture in the back seat, still clutching the reins. How I laughed!

What I really liked was driving the big hard-mouthed carriage horse from the coachman's box, twirling the whip in approved style, especially on the country roads round Oxford. They were not tarred yet and no doubt the carriage wheels stirred up dust or mud. But what did this even more were the early motor cars which we were beginning to see towards the end of the first decade of the century.* I used to shout at them 'Paap-paap! Stinker!' Probably they were quite used to that. Bicycle traffic was growing steadily, but my mother, again, was not keen that I should learn, having some obscure fear that it might damage my sexual organs. I ended, annoyingly, not able to ride a bike, though this was partly because when, in 1914, I at last had one and had begun to learn to ride it, the war came and with it the Belgian refugees. In a flood of sentiment I gave my bike to a girl called Yvonne. In theory it was a loan, but in practice, of course, not. She gave me a rather badly made flowered dress with a lacing of yellow ribbons. But my bike was gone.

* Jack's 1902 diary: they had been driving from Glencraig colliery near Loch Leven. Jack had been down with Uffer and writes full and interesting notes, showing the main differences between a colliery and a Cornish tin mine. Then Mr Wilson, the 'proprietor' of the mine, drove them back through the Yetts of Muckhart where the car began to heat and they had tea at Kippen while it cooled down: 'We didn't break the law badly, as we only once, I believe, reached 24 miles an hour! However we averaged about 17 on level ground.'

In time of course, we ourselves succumbed to buying a car, partly so as to get my father to the station quicker. He was by now going up and down to London fairly often, as a Gas Referee and also in connection with various Government enquiries and Royal Commissions. These meant a special black briefcase as well as many pencils and notebooks, in some of which I wrote my early novels later on. One got the feeling from his anger, talking things over with my mother, that the Home Office constantly had to be prodded into making any kind of move over industrial safety. Probably this was so. I think by this time, too, he may have been starting some connection with Birmingham.

He was taking longer and longer to lace his boots in the morning; he always wore thick, knitted socks and black laced boots which he carried down to breakfast with him, clonking them at any child on the stairs, and did not start putting them on till he had finished the tea and eggs and bacon and marmalade. They held the train for him at Oxford if they could see the carriage turning almost at a gallop up the station incline. It was clear that a motor car would halve the time. They bought a Daimler in 1913: it was supposed to be the most reliable and of course there was a chauffeur, replacing Crackston who by now was extremely alcoholic. But the chauffeur was called up in 1914 and the car was given, I think, to the Officers' Hospital.

X

Politics and People

I took it for granted that my mother's views on everything were right, including her great worship of the British Empire. In one general election I refused to wear my new red flannel coat because it was the Liberals' colour. My father never spoke of his views—or not till many years later—but I did know that my parroting of her political slogans annoyed him, making him frown and shake one foot. It was many years afterwards and my own political views were then not hers; we were walking up the glen at Cloan together, and he said, 'You can imagine what was said when I married an Edinburgh Tory.' I don't propose to consider what 'being in love' is or was, but I believe this had happened to him. I also think that she had made some kind of agreement with him about not expressing his political views. However, as a child, I put enormous enthusiasm into trying to understand hers and if possible going one better. This is clear from the diaries after about 1906.

There would be political pamphlets which I could put into envelopes or deliver to the neighbours. I remember collecting for some earthquake fund—in the West Indies perhaps?—and saying 'They are people like us.' That is to say not mere natives. However, this was not entirely a matter of colour. When the Russo-Japanese war got into the British press, several of the boys at the Dragon School, including my brother, drafted a letter to show their sympathy with the brave little Japs. No doubt this was a matter of un-sympathy with our rivals or enemies, the Russians, whom we thought of as bearlike and constantly throwing babies out of sledges to feed the ravening wolves of the boundless steppes. Now, I wanted to sign the letter too; I must have been six and it was a real matter of status. So they all questioned me on what I knew about the war. I had heard so much that my answers were thought adequate and I was allowed to sign. In due course a letter came back, I suppose from the Japanese Embassy, and was taken in triumph to school to be handed round and admired.

From here came playing Japs. I quote from a 1905 letter, describing yet another happy day with the Slessors. 'We went down to the towpath at Iffley & played Japs . . . & went on board an old barge . . . & played murderers after tea—black crape masks, cloaks & slouch hats.' I feel fairly certain that murderers were envisaged as having daggers or possibly garotting their victims— all very hand-to-hand.

My mother was Oxford's staunchest pillar of the Victoria League, which was in those days much more actively political in the sense of being British Empire orientated, and probably part of Conservative Party background, though it also organised some hospitality, which is its main function today. Among other activities it held an annual bazaar; here I went around in my best frock with a tray of sweets to sell, and I was allowed to buy things for my museum, kauri gum from New Zealand, Zulu beads, a tiny birch bark canoe from Canada, treasures of all sorts. I am sure I was given the money specially, as I had no pocket money until much later; it wasn't at all universal for school children.

One got tips from uncles, but these were usually saved up for something special. Uncle Richard—Haldane of Cloan—used to give Boy a golden half sovereign and me the same when I was past childhood. But I was well aware of my mother's deep political disapproval of him, which I now find sad because I am almost sure he realised that she was remarkably intelligent and he treasured intelligent female company; but he never got near having a rational political discussion with her. He must have found my political imitations of her views singularly trying. I note these from time to time in the later diaries, where there is much about Empire, Compulsory Military Service and similar subjects; I never had any doubts on the correctness of her and my views, though I now find myself unreasonably ashamed and embarrassed when I re-read

85

them. Had I arrived at this earlier, the later break might have been less painful.

Uncle Richard and Aunt Bay were Liberals and in practice deep in party politics. The Liberals were then an official and powerful party, against what they considered Conservative privilege and injustice. The voters (no women) were sufficiently evenly divided for alternate governments to take power, so that there was a democratic structure. Although most of the old traditional upper class were Conservative, with a few mavericks, below that it split class-wise. Today the two old parties may look much the same; it was, for instance, only the radical wing of the Liberals that was genuinely anti-imperialist.

But there was a real difference of opinion over Ireland, where the Conservatives approved of using force to put down 'rebels', while the Liberals favoured reasonable, unarmed discussion, though perhaps with almost the same end in mind. But it was a difference of approach and that was perhaps the dividing line elsewhere. As a child I would always be pleased to hear that we had 'sent a gunboat' to 'show the flag' to dissidents. Oddly enough, this type of phrase is still used emotively to justify enormous expenditure on armaments and still gets the childish response. My mother would accuse her Liberal relations of having caused the death of Britons by not immediately sending soldiers to enforce British rule. Gladstone, the G.O.M. (Grand Old Man) could be called the M.O.G. (Murderer of Gordon). I remember repeating this gibe to my father who responded with pain and anger that scared me into silence.

The other dividing line that I remember was between Free Trade and Tariff Reform, the latter being, I think, Imperial Preference, helping to build up Australian wool and New Zealand butter. Again, people felt passionately about it, though the main thing that sticks in my mind is a Liberal slogan: Tariff Reform means happier Dukes. Presumably, too, the Labour Party was lifting its ugly head. And yet I think my mother and quite a number of fellow Tories would have been as much in favour as any Liberal of social legislation for the amending of obviously bad conditions of work or housing. But for both main parties it was done benevolently, from above. The same was true of education. Board Schools should be improved but they were different in kind from the schools to which one's own children went.

The Victoria League meant parties for Rhodes scholars, who might well find themselves rather friendless, considering how far from home most of them were. But, for my mother at least, they must be suitable ones. She did not, for instance, like Afrikaner accents. But young Fairbridge, with his child emigration schemes, was one of her favourites; the Fairbridge farm schools probably owe much to her backing. I am almost sure that, with hindsight, I am being unfair about this. Let me add that her feminism was very real. She always supported women in the professions, went to a woman doctor when possible and encouraged me to think of medicine as a career. But this was somewhat marred by the counter-force of being a lady. Thus, it was wrong that women should not have the vote, but suffragettes had behaved in a deeply unladylike way. She was therefore a *suffragist*.

It is hard to be accurate or dispassionate about all this. It seems that my father was a quiet Liberal, only drawn into direct politics over an occasional issue such as the Boer War, but in general a believer in social justice, naturally on his own valuation. Like many honourable men he was not 'advanced' in the permissive society sense; he was much easier to shock than my mother was, though this only became apparent to me at a later stage in my life.

It seems also that my mother was an active and constant propagandist for Tory imperialism, as exemplified by Chamberlain, Kipling, her uncle General Keatinge and many public figures of the time. This comes constantly into my brother's diaries: clearly she took him with her whenever possible to League of the Empire meetings, especially those for children or young people, where she spoke and showed 'things from the colonies', including Samoan war clubs and kava bowls brought back by her father (the best of which are now in the Pitt Rivers Museum), Canadian birch bark models, African beadwork and so on. I don't remember any of this but it sounds as if she was a highly competent speaker. Jack in his 1902 diary writes: 'Mother told us very much what is put in the papers,

87

that it is a society for making people more able to fight for their country, and to be useful if they emigrate to the colonies, & to let them know about colonial life by a system of couples of correspondents in England and a colony, or two colonies, and that the Empire isn't a lot of little countries, but one big one, in fact to teach them to be good citizens of the Empire. We enrolled about 10.' Some of these were 'village boys and girls' for whom he had a certain contempt, less social than intellectual—even in Scotland the village school wasn't up to the Dragons!

This reminds me of a laborious correspondence I had with a girl in Mauritius whom I finally met many, many years later. She was one of a huge French family, few of whom had managed to get married; it was all rather sad.

My mother's desk at Oxford was large, with locked drawers, and a great many sheets of facts and figures of the kind with which we propagandists are all too familiar. Clearly she was completely successful with both her children. In Jack's ten-year-old diary he says: 'My mater and I are very sorry to hear of Mr Chamberlain's resignation but hope he will get into office again soon.' Indeed I think there is evidence that he was even more deeply involved in her politics than I was which of course made the inevitable break all the more painful.

Did the fact that we loved her and she—not of course deliberately—used this to bring us into her line of feeling (naturally for what she thought was right and noble) make us more bitter when the time of disagreement came? What else, considering her deep involvement, could she have done with her loved children? And what, I ask you, parents or children, is the moral of that?

She had, meanwhile, a cousin, Charles ffoulkes, who was a somewhat unsuccessful artist and lived with his mother in a house at the corner of Bevington Road. I am sure he sympathised with my mother's political views. He did a lot of work in copper and bronze, good craftsmanship, all of it; he knew a great deal about armour and organised all that side of the Oxford pageant: he bound books. Today such of his work as survives is very fashionable, as it was the better kind of *art nouveau*; he also did drawings for me when I was ill and, I think, helped over the many difficulties that followed my parents' unwise decision not to employ a real architect for their new house, Cherwell, at the end of Linton Road, but instead a building contractor who claimed to be an architect. Gardiner his name was, another of the baddies. But my father disliked Charles ffoulkes; I think he was somewhat jealous and probably my mother did get some affection and sympathy of a kind which she needed from Charlie. His workshop was a very nice place, but I couldn't bear Aunt Annie, his mother, who had probably kept him, her only son, from marrying. He taught me to make chains of butterflies and little people out of folded paper and to make paper dresses for cardboard dolls which had lovely faces when he painted them up, but not when I did.

Oxford held plenty of my mother's fellow imperialists, including believers in the League of the Empire, more political than the Victoria League, with a constant flow of pamphlets which I read eagerly and distributed. Many were non-University people, like the Slessors. They had, I thought, nicer houses than ours, first up Woodstock Road, then Iffley Road. This was almost certainly because they had newer furniture and curtains and light fittings. I liked things new and shiny, in spite of or perhaps because of, my Morris upbringing. At the Hale Whites' house in Harley Street, where Sir William practised as a consultant, my mother and I had a room with shiningly polished wooden bedsteads with curved ends, no iron frames and knobs; they had new, glistening, silk-covered quilts; the dressing-table had a glass top and three mirrors and there were meringues for lunch. Dear Lady Hale White always insisted that I should have a second.

Another nice house was Miss Townshend's up Banbury Road; it was built a decade or so after St Margaret's Road on a much pleasanter plan, with no basement or top floor and the garden had a mound at the bottom nicely planted with rock shrubs and rareties, while in front a thick shrubbery shut off the traffic. Miss Townshend was Irish, wrote fairy tales and did one book with a photo of me as the frontispiece. She told stories and induced me to help with them, and there was an Indian hanging in her drawing-room with a great tree and quantities of beasts and birds among the branches. Here again I was neither talked down to nor owned.

When, at eleven or twelve, I became a serious field botanist and member of the Wild Flower Society, I used to go and visit Mr Druce, the great authority. He had a highly reputable chemist's shop in the High, and round his North Oxford house a garden wholly taken up with wild flowers. He was very kind to me and when, in my early teens, I found one of the *Muscari* in the middle of a spruce plantation, he put it under my name into the Berkshire flora. What happiness!

Naturally, Mr Druce was his own gardener, though perhaps he had someone to cut the lawn. Most professional class people had gardeners and consequently were much less knowledgable and interested than the same social group are nowadays, when they do it all, or most of it, themselves. Among the owners of great gardens, there were a few, fortunately perhaps, who were keen landscapers, planters and breeders, with equally keen gardeners, but others did little but show off their gardeners' work. The real difference was among those with small gardens, who nowadays produce such fine and often unexpected results. Many plants which we grow fairly easily were supposed to be tender or difficult; there were few viburnums other than *laurustinus*; I don't remember the early species crocus or winter cyclamens. Admirers of Morris felt that bedding-out was vulgar, though I loved the flower clock in Prince's Street Gardens in Edinburgh, as surely all right-thinking children must. I doubt if there were many of the really good rhododendrons at Cloan, but it would have been too cold for most of them. But it was in the conservatory, there that I started eating fuchsia berries, not quite so nice now, perhaps, as they used to be.

Our Oxford next-door neighbours on one side of 4 St Margaret's Road had a boy and a dachshund with whom I was vaguely friends, so that we met across the wall, but on the other side were the Murrays in a much bigger house and garden, but I was not supposed to climb in because they were Liberals. This was an emotive word, like Communist is now in some countries or to some people, and had no real meaning for me. Later it faded away; probably by then my mother had come to the conclusion that there were worse bogeys than Liberals. I went back to the house in my late teens and did a few thought-reading experiments with Gilbert Murray; my father thought they were nonsense, but I didn't. Once he caught what I was thinking but said it came out of a Russian novel; he may have got that by picking up the image in my mind which I was concentrating on in the same way I would have done if I had been writing it. It would have been fascinating to go on, perhaps getting in tune with him, but he found it extremely exhausting, as people who can do these things usually find it. Much later my mother and Lady Mary Murray seem somehow to have made friends.

There were always a few people who had something special which made me look forward to seeing them: Miss Legge and her Asian curios, most of which, I believe, ended in the Pitt Rivers Museum: Alice Raleigh and her delicate drawings—she lived in London Place when there was still a block of slummy, elderly houses between her and the main road and there was no inside WC, so I thought she ought to feel poor and unhappy, though I don't think she did. In one letter I had been to tea there and had a lovely time sorting buttons. And at Dr Collier's house, there was a bay window, one end of which looked out onto the High. When going into a new house one tended (and indeed I do still) to give it a quick look over for its hide-and-seek possibilities.

Uncle John, the Professor of Physiology, whose hatred of nepotism led him to be very unfair to my father and unforgiven by my mother, lived in a large ugly house in Banbury Road; I found him impressive, partly because he was in a Holman Hunt picture (May Morning), but I was scared of Aunt Ghetal. However, they had a typewriter and occasionally I was allowed to use it. Thus, my ambition of having a typewriter of my own. But this ties up with something I have long forgotten; the presence of 'Aunt Florence'— Florence Buchanan, a distinguished physiologist whom my mother approved of as a feminist, and felt she must look after, since Florence had a detached retina and her sight became increasingly bad. But I disapproved of her because she was unkempt, had large hairs on her face and smelled bad (if I remember hard I get that smell back). She almost always had lunch with us and I am sure she disapproved of me as much as I did of her.

I had school friends in and around Park Town, including Miss Poynter, sister of a then-famous painter, whose home was full of pictures; I used to blow bubbles there, from a big soapy bowl held on my knees. There were the Starks who lived, I think, in St Giles and then moved out to a low, rambling farmhouse at Noke. They had a model railway in the garden, the same gauge as ours, but still more fascinating, since it went over a miniscule lake and through a tunnel. There was a station with various home-made miniatures in it. How the Stark family, Boy and I, used to gloat over the Basset Lowke catalogues of model trains and all that went with them! At Noke, the 1906 diary mentions two hound puppies, 'one black puppy about a foot long, 8 inches high at his head & one foot round, it had short curly heair and it looked like a bear.' Also a pink bunny and a hen with many chickens, 'they were very clever for thier size I caught 3 & put them in a house I made. They imediately got out, I found through a secret passage into the railway cutting!'

The 1909 diary talks of the splendid hiding places at Noke, especially the loft. I hid there long enough to scare all the others most gratifyingly. Jack's schoolmate, J. D. Walker, came out that time and when he was there too 'it is awfully jolly because there are 6 of us all liking the same things, from J.D. at one end & me at the other.'

Beyond the railway was a tangly unpruned orchard where a friendly donkey wandered, while golden plums dropped lushly from old trees. It seemed to me that in order to have enough of them one must start at dawn, so I laid in plenty of plums under my pillow. And then slept on them. They were very ripe. Mrs Stark was dying of open tuberculosis; her dreadful cough rang through the house. I looked with interest at the blood on the handkerchief she held to her mouth. Did that have anything to do with my own TB? I have an idea that we suddenly stopped going there.

I think there was still a certain feeling that gently brought up children should also be made aware of the realities of human suffering, though this was not as strong as it was a generation earlier. My Foswell cousins were regularly taken to visit an old lady at Auchterarder with lupus-cancer of the face; not pretty. We were more familiar than today's children with death, which tended to take place at home rather than in hospital, and certainly with the idea of the sought-after 'good death'. But we were less familiar with killing and genuine violence, and would have been desperately upset by many of today's news items.

Without quite remembering who they were, I know there were families with whom we took Sunday afternoon picnics with wicker picnic baskets and kettles, well up the Cherwell in fields which were then completely remote except for the cows. If we went downstream there was the fun of Maya and me putting our hands over our eyes as we passed the naked University gentlemen bathing at Parson's Pleasure. There were water rats in plenty and sometimes kingfishers; a mile or two up and the river might be blocked with fallen trees, which our New Zealand cousin Rob Makgill helped us to move; there was one, the Great Snag, which took most of the summer, or so it seems now. My father, in shirt sleeves and braces, rowed, and sometimes I was allowed to steer, but was discouraged from the fascinating sport of bumping other boats. Punts came later, when the river was too crowded for rowing boats. But early in the century everyone knew almost everyone else. The Colleges had their boat houses, but there was no casual hiring and we were all affronted when Timms started the hiring business on 'our' river.

One went more rarely on the Upper Thames, but there was one expedition every year, either by boat or carriage. This was to Wytham to eat strawberries. If we drove there we went by a road now blotted out by the by-pass, with gates here and there and children who opened them and to whom we threw pennies. If we came by river we walked past Fair Rosamund's nunnery, and along a raised path between hedges and above road level, no doubt built that way because of the yearly floods. Traditionally one squashed the strawberries with the bottom of a wine glass before digging in.

Every year, too, we went on brambling expeditions, often on the little train to one of the stations beyond Islip where there was waste land with great bramble thickets where we could easily fill our baskets. We got them in our own hedges too, near at hand. Every year there were crab apples and sloes. Have all those splendid hedges been tidied up now, so that there is no longer the great wealth of autumn fruit? Or do people just not bother about it?

XI

Polly and Others

I begin to wonder about our pets, once I had outgrown the mice. I don't think my mother held with them very much: she hated the smell of carnivores. But our desires were strong. There was a fox terrier called Spot about whom I have no fond feeling; he definitely belonged to the males of the family. And there were the white fantail pigeons, who lived in a pigeon house on the top of a pole at St Margaret's Road; Boy used to lie on the ground with maize up his shorts so that the pigeons could wriggle in to get it. Later, at Cherwell, there were more pigeons and different kinds. That was where I first heard the phrase: 'simple, stable Mendelian population'. Rarely, there were red maize grains among the yellow. I collected them for one drawer of a Japanese toy writing desk in which I kept other collections, including my own milk teeth, out of which I intended to make a necklace, but they were too difficult to bore holes in.

For how many years I have forgotten Timothy Titus of Tavistock! And yet he must have occupied my mind during most of out-of-school time for a whole summer. Someone gave me a yellow duckling, the weakling of a batch which would probably not survive in farm conditions. He drooped in my hands, his eyes shut. But we gave him whisky and he never looked back. I think he was imprinted on me; he followed me everywhere round the St Margaret's Road house and garden, first carried, then wriggling upstairs, step after step. I quickly learned to interpret his various duck noises and was only able to support the idea of an almost adult and non-house-trained duck going back to the farmyard by being told that he would be king. The 1904 (six-year-old) diary has pages about Timothy Titus, including a poem beginning,

'There is a duck called Tim
None other equales him.'

and three rather peculiar drawings. Descending to prose, I write,
'Tim has grown very much since he came here. When he came there
was a sort of skin on his beak but it has pealed of now. It is coloured
browny-gray, but his beak is pink. When he is in the garden alone
he usualy squekes, but when we talk to him out of the window he
stops; he follows you about the garden, and when you go into the
house he evan follows there, he some-times goes into the study &
sits in the middle of the floor. Tim always squeaks when he wants
food; the more hungry he is the louder he squeaks. If at tea anybody
puts down on the grass their cup of tea, Tim, before they can see
Tim, begins to drink it.'

It was well after my broken leg that I started to keep guinea pigs.
I was around twelve and it was the first pair, precursors of hundreds, whom I successfully induced to nibble off a wart on the first
finger of my right hand by holding it against the netting where I
usually put carrots. The wart never came back. But the guinea pigs,
whose language, again, I began to interpret and imitate, and their
many descendants, went on far beyond childhood, taking me into
the almost adult world of early genetics.

And then there was Polly! I never thought of Polly as a pet.
Polly was a person and died in my arms. He (we thought he was a
he) was left to us by my cousin Alys Trotter—with whom he had
lived for many years and where I had first got to know him; we
never knew how old he was. He was immensely affectionate and,
I thought, understanding. When I had my broken leg, Polly walked
gently, carefully, so as not to hurt and came to my face and kissed
me with open beak and little soft dry tongue. That was what he did,
or, if he felt exceptionally friendly, he sicked up pellets of food to
offer one. While he was with us I was able to communicate with
the macaws at the Zoo, even the great red and yellow ones (Polly
was blue-green), and get them to respond, to sit on my wrist and
let me tickle them.

Polly did not care for other non-humans and could easily put a

9. 'The Departure Platform' and 'In the Train'. My impressions of railway travellers from the 1909 diary

ghosts & fairies. He has never seen any fairies, but he says he saw 3 ghosts. They were not at all transparent, but he saw a bumble bee fly through a lady walking down a path. None of them were ghosts of dead people; but in two cases the people were in London, & in the other he saw the ghost of a little girl go into a room, dressed in blue, & going after it immediately he saw the real little girl sitting there dressed in white! My Father & Boy fled precipitately as soon as they heard his motor but my mother & I got on with him quite well, we found him silly, but amusing.

10. *A page from the 1909 diary. Scientific scepticism is obviously at odds with my willingness to believe in Andrew Lang's ghosts*

dog or cat to flight by threatening behaviour, dancing up and down with his wings open and yelling. He did not care for the tits hanging upside down on the coconuts outside the drawing-room window and flapped his wings at them too. But he could not see immediately in front of him and if one put a clockwork mouse so that it would run directly in the line of his beak, he would leap upwards with a prodigious squawk. Boy and I knew this was disapproved of, but once or twice we even made him drunk and he became remarkably human, lurching about and talking a lot, though his vocabulary was not very large. He liked to be in on meal times, climbing up one's chair, pulling my hair or nibbling at Maya's specs. Her somewhat disapproving attitude towards pets, especially carnivores, was completely reversed with Polly, who liked best to go round on her shoulder and was forgiven for tearing a piece of lace when holding on or for feeding her ear with food pellets.

What I didn't like was his habit of grinding his beak while I was doing my prep in the dining-room, where his perch was. It may be that he was simply trying to communicate and that he didn't much like the half-dark of the dining-room with only the reading lamp at the desk where I was trying to do Latin translations or, sometimes, playing my Liberty catalogue game. If I put him down on the floor to roam around he would go to the sand tray below his perch and scatter the sand with his beak, which was equally interrupting.

I don't think I had much homework until I was ten or so, but in the top forms we had a lot, usually two hours. It was less homework in today's sense, when the object is to acquire relevant knowledge out of school, than a test of what one knew, to be marked the next day. So one wasn't allowed help. It was Latin prose, French verbs and sentences, counties and rivers, dates. If it was an essay I had no trouble. Arithmetic was worse, especially Euclid. Later I did solid geometry for fun with my brother and found it very pleasurable.

We had lots of exams and I usually enjoyed them. I was extremely competitive and exams set me off like jumping hurdles. Not that I was ever a hurdler! I was useless at school sports, or at organised games, other than the obstacle race. Later, in my early teens, I was in a North Oxford lacrosse team. This was enjoyable, though I remember how, egged on by my mother, I was against their very sensible suggestion of allowing one's gym tunic to finish just above the knee instead of below it. I still either believed in her total rightness in such matters or was afraid of the bother and disapproval if I had to get the tunic altered. Finally it was solved because I was thrown out of the team for playing foul whenever I got excited.

I think, though, that I learned to skate fairly young. Were winters colder then? Probably not, but I remember the meadow at Magdalen frozen over, and Port Meadow too, and the excitement of getting on one's skates and wobbling out and then sailing clear away. Nor was falling too uncomfortable. The floods, preceding the frost, were always something to watch and talk about and compare. Soon I began to realise how much they were doing for the fertility of the water meadows. Port Meadow itself was special at all times; we went there a lot from St Margaret's Road, an easy walk, over the railway bridge, dragging one's feet if a train was in sight so as to be in the very middle of splendid billows of dark smoke; there was a corrugated iron barrier too, to run along with a stick. I was expert with a wooden hoop about my own height and could run in and out of it while I bowled it along. It was Johnny. But a dreadful thing happened. I was bowling in the field near the site of the new house and my little hoop-boy Johnny fell into the river and was carried away, white and calm and round, down stream, and nobody came to rescue him. After that I played no more with hoops.

The canals and the canal boats with their painted castles and flowers were fun. So were the drawbridges, most of all standing on one, holding on, while it was pulled up. We poked endlessly with sticks in canals and ditches. Once Boy and I pulled out a huge river mussel; we watched, fascinated, when we put it into a jar and it gradually opened and extruded a foot. But when finally it died there was no pearl.

One year there was a thrush's nest in one of the pair of small cypresses which finished off the bridge over the 'back area' from the garden door of St Margaret's Road down to the garden itself and the bushes of pink La France roses. Once a day I was lifted up to feed the gaping nestlings with small pieces of meat. Later, I thought they knew me. Occasionally we found other birds' nests and watched for the parents; whatever else we collected it was never birds' eggs or stamps, though I had an album full of picture postcards of foreign countries. There were magnificent dragonflies up the Cherwell. Earthworms too were sympathetically viewed.

The diaries are full of animals: my own rabbits and bantams, other people's puppies, the seaside donkeys I rode. When Grannie took a small house on Boar's Hill there were rabbits to track and watch and a new lot of birds, jays and woodpeckers. Even the insects were different; I was observant on moths. And the Cherwell had its own animals, birds and water dwellers; there were water rats all along the banks, going about their business.

House rats, however, got no sympathy. We had great rat-hunts at Cloan, with the cairns, good ratters, and Kaiser, the St Bernard, less agile, as long-stop. We and the Foswells were all armed with sticks and hit one another as often as not. We threw the dead rats into the pigsty and the old sow crunched them up, the rat tails hanging out of her mouth at both sides.

Both parents encouraged scientific curiosity, though there was a rule that we did not talk about anything below the diaphragm at meals. But there were other kinds of curiosity, too. I used to spend much time in the Pitt Rivers Museum, partly with the prehistoric skeletons, with which I was always on good terms, and partly with the anthropology section, but not forgetting the plaster duck with protective coloration. Parts of the museum were unfinished and one could watch the stone-carvers at work on the capitals of the small stone pillars of the gallery, sometimes with a sprig of oak leaves or some such thing which they were perpetuating in stone.

I did not care much for the Ashmolean, except for some of the Pre-Raphaelite pictures: Holman Hunt's 'Dovecot', the rescue of the Christian Martyr by well-combed Britons, 'Home from the Sea', all with the detail one always hoped for in pictures but so often didn't get, and with real, vital colours. Wherever I found them later on, in other galleries, these were the ones I stared and stared at. Rossetti was boring with those stupid-looking girls, but Millais and his gardens were always beautiful and one knew at once what the picture was about. There was only one other picture in the Ashmolean that was satisfactory in the same way; that was Uccello's 'Hunt'. Piero di Cosimo's forest fire, with the good but anxious bear rescuing his cubs, was not yet there; if it had been I would have tugged at anyone's hand to stop and look at it. I was moderately interested in Alfred's jewel, but not at all in the casts of classical sculpture.

The Botanical Gardens were a good place, either from land or going in by boat; at ten or eleven I was an adept stealer of cactus shoots and offsets, hiding them under bread for the swans, then growing them successfully to flowering size. In Magdalen there were the deer to feed and the odd little statues of the virtues and vices round the inner quad to identify, or try to. St John's garden had the best rockery, but New College was of course our own. Boy and I scooted up the forbidden Mound in the garden there, and then not again until the year of our father's centenary, when there were lectures and celebrations at his old laboratory and college, and we came back as ghosts.

For a short time there was a private big game museum about opposite the Radcliffe, which I much liked. I used to go there and try to paint kudus. If there had been anything like a science museum I would have loved it. I don't remember being taken to museums in London, only to Madame Tussaud's where I was scared stiff—here were serried nightmares, dead but almost alive. We did go to the Zoo, several times, in the days when, for a small tip, the keepers took out the kinkajous to climb round our necks, or the beautiful, ripple-bodied snakes. We knew what not to give the animals to eat and probably did no harm.

In Edinburgh my great treat was the *camera oscura* in High Street, where, on a great round magic sheet one could watch the moving people, tiny and coloured. But again I don't remember being taken to any museums, though I was sometimes taken to the National Gallery and always wanted to see Paton's 'Oberon and Titania', with all the fairies, good and bad, and again, again, the clear detail. It is again becoming fashionable, but oddly, it has become quite a small picture; I remember it as very big.

XII

The Underpinning

While my mother's father was still alive, that is, before I was seven, the Edinburgh family and servants used to take a house each holiday somewhere in the Lothians. These would be two-storey houses with spacious rooms, a good garden including a kitchen garden and perhaps a conservatory where I was not allowed to pick the flowers. There must, above all, be plenty of opportunities for nice drives. I think my mother was totally bored; her role appeared to be that of dutiful daughter helping with the housekeeping and servants, writing notes; sometimes she and her mother played cribbage; I might be called in to help with winding a skein of silk or wool, holding it between my hands while my grandmother wound. Grandpapa had considerable correspondence, I think about geography; he was a member of several learned societies. There were occasional distinguished visitors. It seems almost certain that Grandpapa took his own horses and trusted coachman, but I remember being taken by the more interesting train.

One house was at Inveresk. I was not allowed to dam any of the streams or set foot in the Esk, already much polluted from the paper mills. Nor was I allowed to play on the sand at North Berwick for the same reason. In fact, we were getting into the modern world. All this comes into the 1904 and 1905 diaries. There were walks to the churchyard 'where some tomb stones have been left lying about'. There were expeditions, for instance to Stirling by boat, going under the Forth Bridge, and an attempt to get to the Belhaven sands past the 'drainy, rocky' Dunbar beach. Later Sina and I went there, or to the Portobello pier, or to fish—there is a drawing of a flounder. There was one great expedition to the Bass

Rock which takes pages of the diary, what with the engine of the launch that took us there, the sea birds, the landing ('not as difficult as landing on the Longships') and the lighthouse mechanisms. Other expeditions were to Dalkeith, Rosslyn, to Miss Wauchope 'who has been all over the world', to a flower show at Pinkie, and to Miss Wardrop who had a pony called Mysie 'which I drove myself; I do like driving with Mysie in a pony cart'. I fed her with apples and rode her, more or less.

On both years when Grannie and Grandpapa were at Inveresk we drove over to Preston Pans. The salt pans where the sea water was evaporated were still there and still one got the big scrunchy crystals of Sunday salt when the evaporation went on over the Sabbath. But there was also the Preston Pans pottery, where I was allowed to make a clay bowl on a wheel and to buy myself a penny money box shaped like a monkey. The 1904 diary goes into the industrial process with great care, starting with the clay ('I have seen white clay works near Penzance'), going on to, 'They used to make more interesting things than teapots & pie dishes, they showed us an old china man, he was 300 years old and beautifully painted. They smash a awfull lot of things, and through the broken bits onto the shore, when mother heard this she turned round like a —— and said "to cut the children's feet upon!" '

There was also Cockenzie House where Colonel Cadell and his daughters lived. That was the best place. There was a long drawing-room stretching right across the house. As I remember, one window looked north over the harbour with storms louring and wind and fishing boats and bustle, and the other south over the garden with clipped hedges and richly flowering roses in quiet sunshine and white fantails parading on green grass. Between the windows were cabinets, one with mirrors at the back, tortoiseshell panels and little inlaid drawers; there was fine china behind glass; there was ivory and sandalwood, camphorwood chests and worked brass from India; there were pictures, which I liked, also full of storms and sunshine—early Cadells perhaps, for this distinguished Scottish painter was first cousin once removed to the Colonel. And above, running the length of the house, was a corridor with a springdale, a thin board that one sat on and it jumped one up. In the garden a swing was set between ivy-run whales' jawbones and a white marble Nandi, an Indian temple or palace bull, reclined calmly in a very Scottish grotto.*

All this and more comes into the diaries. There is a drawing of the springdale. But the most enthusiastic description is in 1908 when we actually stayed there, and now I recall Colonel Cadell feeding the black and white fantails that crowded onto his head and shoulders, though I don't remember the Persian cats. Nor yet the 'great collection of daggers, taken from Indian convicts, each of which is said to have murdered at least one man', nor even the Indian prince's baby clothes given by the Maharani of Ulwar. There was an Indian inlaid jewel case and a long sword, as well as things from the Nicobars. Colonel Cadell had been Governor of the Andamans, where he and his daughters had rowed out to caves full of the edible swifts' nests, which had never been visited before, so that the swifts were quite tame and could be stroked; one supposes that is all over now. The Miss Findlaters were there too, 'authoresses whose books I have seen reviewed in Punch'.

We stayed at Woodhouselea where the 'walls are quite 8 feet thick' with the Fraser Tytlers; it is a notoriously haunted house, but that kind of haunting didn't bother me. Trotters and Fraser Tytlers had been friends for five generations and my mother and

---

* Jack's diary tells a lot more about the bull, which had been brought over by Colonel Cadell's brother who was a gunner and was able to take it away on his gun carriage, presumably after the 'Mutiny' in which Colonel Cadell won his V.C. It is of course taken for granted that loot is loot. He goes on, 'As soon as the bull was safely installed at Cockenzie, a letter came from the Duke of Somerset's son, saying the bull was his property! He declared that the Colonel of the 17th Lancers had given it to him, however on investigation it was found that he had *asked* the Colonel if he could take it, and as no-one else wanted it, his request was granted. However, having no gun carriage, he was unable to take him away, and Capt. Cadell of the artillery, who came next, bagged it, and by the laws of loot, it belonged to the man who could carry it off. The Duke of Somerset's son then wrote for "his bull" to Captain Cadell who replied that he had given it to his father. Old Commander Cadell was then asked by the Duke of Somerset to name his legal adviser; he replied that that was a luxury in which he could not afford to indulge, and also that he knew more of the laws of loot than any London lawyer! So the bull remains at Cockenzie in a grotto built of lava from Hekla, brought home by herring boats as ballast.' Those were the days.

'Aunt Christian', who had been a Kerr, tended to have second sight about whatever the other one was doing or thinking. I painted the trunk of a tree with just one branch sticking out and called it 'Last of the Kings of the Forest'. That was really rather grand! I think I only liked painting flowers and plants, which led me to look at them rather carefully. At Inveresk there were begonias in the conservatory, some with stamens, others with the curiously convoluted style which is typical; these I immortalised at six in coloured chalk, a he begonia and a she begonia.

We may have stayed with the cousins my mother loved at Colinton among the lawns and great sixty-foot holly hedges against which the summer annuals blazed. But I remember it as gloomy, the end foreshadowed. There were other houses near Edinburgh with relations or friends, and so often one of them was a bit 'wowffy'. There was a very fair girl a little older than me with epilepsy—but what was that? I wasn't told.

By now my brother was in his teens and had got over the worst of his early time at Eton; he did the normal upper-class things, rode, shot—quite well—and, apparently, was a fairly good boxer. There were various boy cousins and I suppose my mother was beginning to think of a suitable match for me. But I remember none of them and few survived the first war.

From Cloan we visited a few big houses. Miss Christie had a Japanese garden with all the trimmings, a little bridge and a temple, incongruously set in a Highland landscape where the view was all wrong. And everywhere we went there was the accepted underpinning of servants. This might mean a happy and comfortable relationship, probably on both sides, as it usually seems to have been at Cloan. The servants were almost always local people, their parents respected and often intelligent members of the same church. There was never any need to lock things up, as one might have to do elsewhere.

It was a funny business, really. Here were people living in the same house, walking through the same rooms, but thought of differently. Yet isn't this to some extent true of all groups? People give one another different kinds of understanding. Scrubbing and emptying other people's chamber pots were thought of as inferior work, but it led to higher things and one could only admire skilled ironing and pleating or silver cleaning, and the upper servants at least would, in Scotland, have insisted on a relation of mutual respect and would never have stood for impertinence by the young. And again, when we think back to a set-up of nominal—at least—servants and masters, we have to remember that what seems odd and even shocking today, was not so yesterday. We can't be sure which of the actions and habits and relationships of today will seem all wrong tomorrow; don't let's be too certain who to blame for what. Sixty years ago, a young girl and her parents were probably very happy when she was taken 'into service' at Cloan where perhaps her mother had been before her; she learnt a number of skills and was proud of them; she had a position; she had friends. That was what mattered.

But even so the servants were different. Formal relationships were entailed; from babyhood, almost, I was Miss Naomi, putting a distance between us. If a new kitchen maid came she was watched and commented on; she might be discussed between Granniema or Aunt Bay and Mrs Cook, like allied generals. And of course the servants had their domain, into which one didn't go unless invited—or at one's peril, the main peril being that the grown-ups on one's own side of the boundary might be told and then one was in for a scolding—worse if one was a boy.

The servants exerted a powerful influence on the household, perhaps stronger than was ever admitted. Sabbath-keeping became increasingly something one did as an example to the servants, though some of the adults still believed in it—but perhaps in a different sense. Certainly the servants imposed ideas on the children whom they saw most of, though sensible children might translate the language when talking it back to their mothers. These would be class ideas, what was 'common'. They enhanced the ideas of ladyhood and what was expected of one, and the unwritten rules. From below, one was told that one must not descend.

Sometimes we went to other large houses where there were real nannies. Sina was not in any sense a 'nanny'; she did not have complete charge, nor was she a mother substitute, but I was very fond of her and so, I think, was Jack. These others were more formidable than ordinary grown-ups: grace was said, which made me uncomfortable, and there was insistence on table manners. I was always offended if I had to have a 'nursery' meal; my status was being questioned. And I was certain the grown-ups who had brought me were having something lovely, like roast chicken or hot-house grapes, while we had boiled fowl and milk pudding.

But there were other odd things. Here for instance is an incident from slightly later. I was having a bath and forgot to bolt the door. The then-butler almost came in, but stopped as soon as he became aware there was someone towelling; I thought it funny and made some remark to Maya. Her reaction was 'Did he see you? If so he must leave the house at once!' Of course he didn't, I said, yes, I'm sure, no, of course not, and so on. I was horrified at this threat held over the poor man who had in fact merely and innocently opened a door a few inches. Nor could I really see what this new fuss was about. But it was a lesson to me—not to talk.

There was a staircase at Cloan, leading up from near the back door to the servants' bedrooms. I never went up and I doubt if Granniema would have gone up except in case of dire illness or some similar mishap. I tried to guess at the rooms by counting the windows from the outside, but could never be sure. In the new house at Oxford, built 1905–1906, there was a servants' flat at the top with its own bathroom. It had a door which opened into the schoolroom and I knew it fairly well, as I often ran down that way, going by the back stairs to avoid those I might meet on the front ones. The rooms were under the roof with sloping ceilings, but were very nice, with gorgeous views over the river. My daughter had it as a flat in the fifties and sixties. Two of the bedrooms certainly were meant to be shared. There was a servants' hall below, opposite the kitchen, which also held the linen cupboard. It seemed quite a friendly place and I knew more or less what went on in that world by then. But I still never did any cooking.

The bigger the house, the higher the barrier. But one must modify this in one way. In the one-servant house with the 'slavey', usually young and easily put upon, sometimes old and cross, there must have been a really cruel barrier, isolating the wretched woman and asserting the superiority of the employer. But I don't think I knew any such households. Later, of course, the household with a single 'help' was common, but by then, already, the relationship had changed.

At Cloan the barrier meant a certain provocation to raiding from our side, when one of us took a dash into Tom Tiddler's Ground usually for goodies of some kind, though it was more practical to be on friendly terms with Mrs Cook or, for grown-up dinner party leftovers, with the butler. I suppose Granniema, or, later, Aunt Bay, had daily discussions, talked over meals, though not necessarily in detail, and the state of the stores. Aunt Bay certainly did the books—going over the household accounts at her desk, where she was also writing the life of Descartes.

My mother did the same. It was careful accounting, down to the halfpennies, with everything she had spent. I rather think that my parents had a joint account at an Oxford bank in the High where people behind counters weighed and shovelled shining pennies and half-crowns, but my mother had a personal account at Coutts where the ladies of the Trotter family have banked for a couple of hundred years and where I and my daughters, equally, keep our accounts.

My mother had a bunch of keys and was always locking things up. This is not a compulsion I have inherited. I think she was always more suspicious of her servants who were, after all, English. How happy she was that the furniture removal men, who brought the things down from Edinburgh after my grandfather's death, were Scots! A Scottish accent in the lower classes meant a proper attitude: not fawning but knowing what was what. Both she and my father were sometimes taken in by hard cases with Scots tongues in their heads. My own accent was groomed to upper-class standards, a pity in these days when a regional accent is such an asset for TV or radio! All that is left of my native country is that I pronounce both letters in 'wh' and 'ch' and 'r' sound in mid-word are still perceptible. Oddly enough my mother herself used certain

Scotticisms which I inherited, ashet, gigot, redd, for instance. Often I deliberately use 'will' instead of the English 'shall' when it seems to sound better in a sentence.

Oxford servants were much discussed in drawing-rooms. If one didn't have some kind of local source, like farmers' daughters, whom one might know something about, then there was nothing for it but a registry office. Then there was the business of written references and reading between the lines. What had been left out? Ladies were often asked for references for someone who had been with them years before, if, say, the most recent employer had died.

I think most Oxford households tended to have a relationship with some professional waitress who came in to help for a big do of any kind. Such people were also in demand for College garden parties or children's Christmas parties, where extra help was needed. After World War One this kind of thing probably increased, as regular parlour maids became fewer and more expensive, but Miss Williamson's coming in was a fairly early memory and my mother's relief when she turned up, took off her hat and coat and took charge. She was always 'Miss' which showed she was not a servant but could be trusted. She saw to the silver and the table setting and dealt with any little *contretemps* like my father gazing absentmindedly at a joint or bird and forgetting to carve. When there was no butler she saw to it that the right wines went into the right glasses.

These were mostly grown-up dinner parties, to which I didn't go till much later, but Miss Williamson could sometimes be found at New College or other parties, and would manage to slip me that extra ice or bit of cake. We ourselves had a garden party once every summer at least. It was the Oxford thing to do and was a good way of polishing people off. The ladies wore frothy dresses, big hats and white gloves, the men often looked cool in white flannels and there were usually other children. I expect the idea was to have it at a time when the garden looked nicest, but the garden at St Margaret's Road was small and the garden at Cherwell not very imaginative or well laid out. My mother was much more interested in the vegetables than the flowers! Its chief merit was some fine walnut trees.

Some years these produced massively and we picked baskets and baskets of walnuts and I was perpetually stained with walnut juice. In one of the later World War One years, chopped walnuts made the flour nicer as well as making it go further.

We had various gardeners who came in, but none were friends. I did a lot of weeding and also berry picking. There were more varieties of strawberries and gooseberries at that time, both in gardens and for sale, but the raspberries, though flavoury, had more caterpillars in them. I don't remember nearly as many winter-flowering plants, nor were there more than a few iris hybrids. I doubt if the species iris or tulips were grown. Probably the College gardens were well ahead of the dons' gardens when it came to new or difficult plants.

My father usually dined in College on Sunday evening, rather a relief perhaps, because we tended to have quite a lot of undergraduates coming in for Sunday tea. This meant the silver tray and tea set, including the hot water urn with the little lamp lighted below it and the silver dish for the hot buttered scones. The silver was polished by the parlour maid into a real glitter with plate polish; there was no 'long-lasting'. Knives were ground in a knife machine with a handle one turned round. Napkins were folded, either plain mitre shape for ordinary meals, or into various fancy shapes for a party. An experienced parlourmaid was good at this.

I got a lot of fun from the damask tablecloths and napkins to match. Sometimes I even helped to set them on the polished mahogany table over, I think, a green baize foundation. Maya wasn't good at flower arrangement, and when I left school and she got a governess for me, I know she was interested in Miss Blockey's ability to 'do' the flowers. However I very soon took that on myself. We had a kind of Victorian mosaic tray in the drawing-room, inherited from Randolph Crescent, where Granny used to have azaleas in pots on it, which seemed to me the height of luxury. It would take pot plants or else large jars in the middle with smaller ones on the outside. In fact it was remarkably ugly and I did not grudge it later on to Sotheby's.

We are so accustomed to certain kinds of conveniences and

gadgets that, in Euro-America at least, we have rather forgotten what things were like before. There was, of course, no mechanical help in the kitchen nor with washing. Servants were used to going on their knees and scrubbing floors. It was the period before disposables. Soap is harder to wash out of one's hair than a shampoo! When I began to menstruate, rather early and alarmingly, for I had not taken in any of the tactful hints which my mother had made on the subject, there were no disposable sanitary towels. They were made of towelling or thick linen damask and one had to learn to fold them into a kind of pocket. When finished with, one rolled them up, put their own loop round them and dropped them into the dirty clothes basket. I *think* they went to a laundry at the end of the week and were soaked in cold water, for the stains came out of them. But it must have been someone's job to undo and sort them. Probably things like stained knicker linings were washed at home. But not by the wearer.

This seems now to be strangely barbarous. But we took it for granted and so, on the other side of the dividing line, did they.

XIII

The Doings of the Grown-ups

Breakfast at Cloan always started with porridge—good porridge made with salt—and sometimes cream. Following tradition we supped it standing, which meant we could observe the grown-ups and even read their letters over their shoulders. The most interesting of the grown-ups was Uncle Richard, though we had to be a little careful about breathing down his neck; he could scatter us. His correspondence came in large, stiff new envelopes with the lion and unicorn on the back and big red seals. These were real seals, none of your phony wafers. One learnt young, in the days before sellotape, to seal a parcel or letter securely and tidily, spreading the wax in a nice round pool, then quickly, before it hardened, pressing down the well-licked seal for just long enough. Many people had seal rings; my father's was a gold seal with his coat of arms, my mother, being an heiress, that is an only child, having hers quartered on his. I have forgotten it all now, but at eight or nine I was fascinated by heraldry, the words and the usages. Charlie ffoulkes taught me all this and gave me the books. I could reel off the rigmaroles and amused myself making up 'correct' coats of arms for my friends. It blended in, too, with *Idylls of the King*, which was my favourite reading aloud at that period.

But of course the best seal of all, with the coat of arms which I knew by heart, was the Great Seal of England, with which we became familiar. As Lord Chancellor, Uncle Richard had to take the Great Seal about with him under his personal charge. I suppose he got a direct sleeper from London to Crieff Junction, now Gleneagles and steadily going down in the world, fewer trains stopping, fewer flowers and less paint. He would have had to have at least one meal on the train, and had to carry along to the dining-car the case with the Great Seal in it, which looked light, but wasn't. Then it lived in his room at Cloan.

When a document actually had to be sealed, the man whose job it was, the keeper perhaps, came up in a neat business suit, but with a mysterious bag like a doctor. We all went off to the old laundry, for this was a messy business. Any piles of sheets were cleared into a corner and made to wait.

The procedure was for a large cake of wax, red or green, depending on the kind of document, to be thoroughly soaped. There was usually a silk cord to be passed through the seal and in fact I think it was done with two cakes pressed together. The seal itself was fitted face down into a kind of screw press, the wax was heated on a small burner and the screw turned down until the wax was squashed and the soap bubbled out. This was always a pleasure and we were given bits of wax—just the thing, naturally, for my museum.

This cannot have been before 1911, so it is not really a childhood memory, but I seem to have had the same direct visual appreciation of the scene; I remember the smell of the wax. Uncle Richard also brought back some of the expensive things Lord Chancellors had to buy, especially the embroidered purse, which hung on a chair back. But on his second term he managed to start the custom that these were to be handed over to the successor, thus saving future Lord Chancellors a considerable sum.

One of my father's colleagues, Professor Boyes, one of the other Gas Referees, knew all about soap films and had invented a cup which could be twirled round on a stem; one drew a thin film of soap across it and as one spun it the colours ran into exquisite tiny patterns of blobs and whirls. In the middle where it was thinnest a dark area gradually developed and spread until the whole film collapsed. I played with this for hours, as also with a kind of simple wooden pantograph which produced patterns which seemed to me to relate to the soap films.

But what exactly were the grown-ups? Another version of Them? Something not quite understood and therefore frightening as well as having authority? One could dodge and outwit, but probably in the end they won. Death the ultimate grown-up? I wonder.

There were some grown-up professions which one supposed one understood; I played orchid-collecting in the Himalayas, especially on the Sennen cliffs. But of course I never thought of the orchids as being objects of commerce. Equally, when I thought about the East India Company with which many of my forbears on my mother's side had been connected, I imagined it as some kind of noble agency, governing and helping the poor Indians. One got the idea, not utterly bad, that one must help those in worse situations than oneself. Uffer, I well knew, worked so hard and was so often in danger to help miners and sewermen and divers. If I had considered the mine owners at all, I suppose I would have taken what is, basically, the Tory point of view, that they had been helping the miners by opening and equipping the pits. But the profit motive entirely escaped me for a long time.

Doctors were simple. So were soldiers and sailors (who were, naturally, always defending the Flag) and civil engineers who built bridges and railways. All science was good, but one must be kind to animals though, regrettably, some scientists weren't. But if one had been in the lab and seen Uffer handling animals, one knew that he was kind. Fairly soon I began to make comparisons between farm practice, especially cattle markets and such things as castration and dehorning, and scientific practice with the cheerful cagefuls of guinea pigs and darling mice.

But I had absolutely no consciousness of economic facts, nor was this even mentioned at school and barely in any history book I read in my teens. None went further than the Diamond Jubilee or possibly the lamented death of Queen Victoria, who had not yet been subjected to any kind of critical process. If one thought about economics at all, it was money, of which some people had more than others. But why? That hadn't occurred to me. I am quite sure this state of mind was common to most upper-class children, most of all the girls. It was all very Freudian in a curious way: money was dirt. It should be no concern of ladies except in such small quantities as not really to count: what would go into a purse was harmless. The difficulty of this point of view is that if and as money must at some point be dealt with, it assumes an unnecessary and ugly importance, like a pile of shit in a drawing-room. Teaching of simple economics would have helped, but there was nothing of the kind in our schooling in those days. Besides, it might have been disturbing.

I don't think I, or any of my contemporaries, ever read a daily newspaper unless there was something very special that we were made to read. Neither of my parents had any use for the 'popular' press, which was considered only fit for the servants (my mother had exactly the same feeling about religion). With no radio, children were far more isolated from world events than they are today. There were no 'current events' or similar school classes. Nor were we aware of the prices of ordinary things; we were taken shopping; we never did it on our own. It was often, however, pleasantly basic and untinned; there was no polythene or plastic problem. I always enjoyed a small shop in the Cornmarket at Oxford where there were great open sacks of flour and maize and other cereals that one could run one's fingers through. At that time, of course, there was a real weekly market at Oxford with beasts driven through the streets; it was very definitely a country market town as well as a university town and remained so until the Morris works started. Elliston's was the big shop, but my 'sensible' shoes came from Free-man, Hardy & Willis at the corner. On the whole we did not take our purchases away; they were delivered at the back door. If a new errand boy unwittingly went to the front door, he was sharply re-proved. In Auchterarder, however, we would pick up the singed sheep's head from the smiddy by the bridge. The only prices I knew at all were for boxes of soldiers or spares for our railway.

Without economics, politics don't mean much. Yet *Harding's Luck*, published in 1909, stirred up the beginnings of political doubt. I think I know when something in the nature of real political illumination happened to me, and it is rather odd. In the interests of my education in my early teens, Maya took me to hear Lansbury and Larkin speak at an Oxford meeting in aid of the Dublin dock strike. I am sure she felt that these were people who were being unfairly treated and whom we ought to 'help', the more so perhaps as it showed that the poor Irish must continue to be looked after by the good English. Yet I think this is unfair; she was never quite as *simpliste* as I have made out. She knew (and disapproved of) the Webbs, but had certainly read some of the early Fabian essays, if only to refute them. Also, her own brand of help could be extremely practical, involving her in personal effort and expenditure. The only criterion seemed to be that whoever was to be helped must show courage in a difficult situation; this again may have been part of the reason why she felt the Irish dockers deserved—something.

So there was certainly for her, at that meeting, an element of philanthropy. But I, for my part, experienced something in the nature of conversion. In tears I put all my pocket money into the collection, a thing I had never felt impelled to do in church.

Historical research was something adults did, especially the Professor—Hume Brown, who at one stage of his career was tutor to the Haldane boys, as well as their sister, Aunt Bay, since she, unusually, shared much of their education. I thought I knew the kind of thing he did and why he didn't want to be interrupted when he was working in the dog-smelling, pipe-smelling library.

From time to time there were theologians and churchmen at Cloan. I remember the fascinating clobber of the two Archbishops, and also how Kaiser, Uncle Richard's beautiful St Bernard, putting up an amiable paw, laddered two pairs of ecclesiastical silk stockings. After that they took to duller gaiters. Kaiser was an immensely friendly dog, but his tail was just on the level of the tea table and a good wag sent the cups flying. I did not much like him in his puppy days, since, true to form, he always wanted someone to rescue and this was usually me, but, to make the rescue plausible, he had to knock me down first, often onto scratchy gravel. Later, when I could swim, I got my own back by dodging him in the chill waters of the dam, or even pulling him round by the tail. In 1914 there was an attempt to change his name to Albert (of the Belgians), but he never responded and maybe there was something in it, for he took to killing sheep. There was the terrible baying that showed he was after one, and we all poured out of the house, trying to stop him. Once, all the same, he charged at a group of black-face tups and one of them knocked him over; black-face tups don't care to be pushed around. He hated being chained, but was given a long wire and ample leash so that he could gallop in the 'Kaiser-feld'.

Later still, I remember Inge, the Gloomy Dean, coming to stay at Cloan, and one evening when I had left my elders to their arguments, but came down afterwards and found my father in a state of deep irritation, jerking his foot as he did when feeling like that, I asked what had happened, and where was the Dean? My father answered, 'I have been trying to teach the elements of Christianity to that man!'

Granniema looked very keenly on the visitors. When she was approaching her century and had taken to her bed, they were summoned to be inspected and talked with. I asked her once what she had thought of Ramsay MacDonald. 'A very agile-minded young man, my dear,' she answered.

It was a pity that my mother's and Aunt Bay's feminism never coalesced, but politics stood in the way, perhaps a touch of jealousy. However, Maya was devoted to Granniema, who enjoyed a certain liveliness in her which did not always come out in the serious Haldanes and Nelsons. Besides, Granniema's immense breadth of human sympathy easily included her daughters-in-law, though neither Maya nor Aunt Edith came to the formal New Year prayers. Nor was I in on them until much later when I was more or less grown up myself.

At this time all Granniema's available descendants, but not the in-laws, gathered at her bedside. Then Uncle Richard addressed the Absolute, explaining what the family had been doing and thinking over the year. After that Granniema asked a blessing on all of us, and we all kissed her. She looked wonderful with her two long white plaits tied with her favourite pink ribbon, her specially knitted bed jacket, and the lace and lightest of Shetland shawls over her head.

Meanwhile in Auchterarder the heidyers and futyers from the two ends of the village met and fought in a perhaps older New Year rite. I could see the lights on the ridge from Granniema's window and wished I was there. But that would not have been the right thing.

The Professor would not have come to the intimate family prayers. Dear Hume Brown, one of the last of the Whig historians of Scotland, what a nice man he was! Among the grown-ups, he was the one who was most likely not to be cross if one asked questions or showed off. He always had his own bedroom kept for him and his special armchairs in the library: the dogs loved him. But there were so many distinguished visitors at Cloan round whom we children skirmished, among dogs, politicians, philosophers, soldiers —Uncle Richard had after all organised both the Expeditionary Force and the Territorial Army in the teeth of Conservative disapproval—scientists and historians. For them the table in the hall was spread with newspapers and learned journals; I dipped into them and sometimes found something I wanted to read. A few, like *Blackwood's*, even had stories. But they had to be put back tidily.

My favourite place was the window-seat in the drawing-room behind the table with the books and the marble doves drinking. One could observe from there and absorb whatever seemed absorbable. Best of all the books, I think, was *Adventures of a Young Naturalist*. The people, chatting away in their grown-up clothes with Aunt Bay and whoever else was there, were somewhat cut off; I seldom wanted to be routed out of my hidey-hole.

There were occasional writers, like Marie Belloc Lowndes, a nice, friendly person, but the only one with whom I had a real friendship was Andrew Lang, although in my 1909 diary, at our first meeting, I found him 'silly but amusing'. We got on much better the next year, when we talked to one another about poetry and he did not, like the rest, snub me when I said that I wanted most of all to be a poet. We also talked about fairies and such. These he encouraged me to see (or think I saw). Looking back on this, it seems to me that what I perhaps perceived, rarely and fleetingly, but most commonly between the ages of about twelve and thirty-five, was as though any present moment of time consisted of something like two sheets of paper, each with a pinhole, moving against one another. If the pinholes accidentally coincided and one happened to be looking, one saw through. This was always interesting and pleasant. Twice, much later, I have seen something of the kind, but once I was in a state of great stress. One doesn't know.

However, all this led to an incident at Oxford where a poor young man from Jesus had written a Ph.D. thesis to prove the existence of fairies, and Andrew asked me to sit in as an expert on the oral examination. It was clear to me that at one point he had mixed up *voler*, to fly, and *voler*, to steal, in the French version of the Fairy Ointment story. But I was very sorry for him and realised how embarrassing it must have been for him to have me there. But what fun for Andrew Lang!

XIV

The Diving Days

I was eight years old when my father did his classic deep diving experiments for the Admiralty in the Kyles of Bute. I remember this patchily, but there is plenty about it in my 1906 diary which starts with the boat trip from Greenock in the *Mercury*, with the long loch and the hills folding and unfolding, and the obsolete battle-ships which were 'waiting in the water for someone to buy them'. The next two days were spent exploring the burns above the hotel at Colintraive where we stayed and about which I have somewhat dubious memories. Highland hotels were not all that good in those days. I know Boy and I played sources of the Nile, going further and further up but never quite getting to where even the smaller burns really began.

The vegetation was very different from Oxford or the Lothians, or even Cloan: dwarf oaks and birches, heather and ling; it might have been more like Cornwall but I had never been at Sennen so late in the year. I was fully aware of these differences and enjoying them. There was high heather and the bracken over my head. Apparently we saw a great many grouse—I wonder if we would now. Then 'we climbed up a quarry but at the top the midges bit so that we came down. Then we went to the beach and watched the barn-acles opening and shutting their shells; a barnacle opens with slits like this.' Here a little pencil drawing of a barnacle. 'When it opens it puts out a little brown arm and sweeps the water in and gets food from the water. I found a shell with water in it and some little beasts were swimming in the water. They looked like tiny slaters, only they were blue. They seemed to be able to swim and to walk, they had a great many legs.'

When one was half one's adult height, that much nearer the surface of things, there was always something near the ground to look at. But what I now remember best were the great nests of the wood ants in the pine woods. There is only a short mention in the diary, but whenever I see them now I go back for a moment to being the me then. We were on the way to a house with a lovely garden sloping down to the sea; from the diary I identify the owners as Mr and Mrs Mackenzie—but what Mackenzies are there now in a lovely garden 'which I think is almost perfect' near Colintraive?

I also remember our expedition to the vitrified fort on Burnt Island. None of the grown-ups seemed to have had an adequate explanation of what a vitrified fort is. Clearly I was fascinated. 'We *all* wanted to take some stone away but we called one another trippers and we did not (except me).' But I was equally fascinated by the hermit crabs which walked about on our hands. At that time we had Arthur Makgill, one of the New Zealand cousins, staying with us. He must have been in his early twenties and I was clearly very devoted. I can just remember playing Consequences with him and finding him exquisitely witty.

Reminded by the diary, I recollect gazing down through very clear water at a wrecked boat with starfish and flat fish 'lying at the bottom and blinking at us'. Clearly there were two expeditions, one by ourselves, the others with the sailors from the *Spanker*, the gunboat sent by the Admiralty for my father's deep diving experiments, with Mr Catto, the diving instructor. 'He says he will take Boy down. I wish I were a boy.' These two expeditions run together in my head, but what I remember best is not even mentioned in the diary. I was steering the sailing cutter between Burnt Island and the wreck, steered too close to the wind, jibbed and the boom swept off the cap of a sailor from the *Spanker*. I was both convulsed with laughter and terrified of having done this both to a grown-up and to an adored sailor. And his cap looked so funny bobbing on the water!

There are pages and pages about the *Spanker*. My father and Boy went off to Rothesay. Maya and I followed the next day by steamer. I remember the smell of dead fish on Rothesay pier and looking over the side to see them in masses at the bottom. Possibly they were herring, which had been dumped by the fishing boats because there was no market for them, but nothing comes into the diary. We went on board and were introduced to the officers and were just in time to see Mr Catto having his diving dress put on. There is a careful description of this old type of diving dress which we got to know so well. My father even had a pipe given to him with the bowl made like a diver's helmet. At the end of the description I say, 'I cannot explain the pumps because I do not understand them, but they are each worked by six sailors turning wheels.' After that we went round with Mr Henson, the first lieutenant, who seems to have shown us everything, starting with the bridge and going on to the conning tower where I seem to have been allowed to work the foghorn. We went on to the anchors. 'I found it was like Earls Court exhibition. It is pulled up by a windlass as they do big sailing boats at Sennen.'

Then we went down to the sailors' quarters, the hammocks and the mess room. Finally we had the 4.7 guns explained. We seem to have gone into it all very thoroughly. Then 'the gunner brought a shell case and the fuse and loaded the gun and we pointed it at a boat which Father did not like at all and he said "Oh, no, wait a minute" but Boy fired! It gave the people in the boat a big jump but it could not have hurt them because there were no shells in the gun. I fired another one. Boy and I ran round to the muzzle of the gun before the nitrous fumes of the cordite came out but Father told us not to breathe it as it was poison. We looked down the inside of the gun and saw the rifling which is for the shell to go through more easily. Mr Catto came up after he had been down two and a half hours. He brought me a sea urchin, two starfish and one whelk, a very large one, all alive. The whelk's aperculum was like tortoiseshell.'

After that 'we had tea in the wardroom which is the dining-room and drawing-room of all the officers except the commander, who has a room all to himself, which must be very dull. Father had tea with him and talked business. Boy slept on board last night beside a row of rifles and pistols and he could reach to draw a dirk from his hammock. Father slept at Rothesay which cannot have been half so nice.' Clearly this was a wonderful day and I end, 'It is very nice to think we are not trippers but have come to Colintraive on business for the Admiralty.'

There is a glimpse of another side of it in a letter from Boy to Grannie. This describes how Uffer, the Owner, and the Bloke dived and then he dived himself. He tells of the pain in his ears which felt as though they were bursting 'but they didn't burst' and then he gets to the bottom, fixes the distance line and explores the bottom. 'The same beautiful light green from the sky down to the dust clouds, or as one should say mud clouds, that one kicked up.' What he doesn't mention is that as he was in a grown-up diving dress the cuffs on the sleeve were much too big for him and the water seeped in so that when he was finally brought up he was in water to the waist. But how I envied him!

There is one other thing I remember very well. It takes a lot of the diary and a drawing. 'We saw a tiny bat hanging on a little tree just outside the front door. It looked like a little mouse with wings. He hung on to the branch with little hooks at the end of his wings. He had Chain Stokes respiration which means that he left off breathing and then went on again. Father timed it and it left off breathing for ten minutes and then went on again. We cut off the branch it was on and put it into a jar. After supper it gradually woke and soon began to walk up the branch. We put in a leaf with green fly on it which it ate and Mother poured in some milk which it drank immediately. We saw its little tongue and its eyes. We put it out and in the morning it had gone.'

From then on we used to see Lieutenant, later Captain, Guy Damant quite often coming for consultations at Oxford. He was part of ordinary life and always willing to join me in my ploys. The deep diving experiments went on as well as those on submarines. Again there was Uffer's acute indignation when someone disobeyed orders, brought a diver up too quickly and let him get 'bends'. Then it was a case of telephone calls and the decompression chamber quick. The Navy had all this taped but it took longer for commercial diving firms to realise what had to be done. Later there was close contact with Siebe Gorman, who built an artificial diving tank where more experiments could be carried out. At the same time there was always work going on to improve mine rescue apparatus and methods. My father's study at Cherwell opened into an inner laboratory and a larger outer one with airtight chambers for work on various gases and pressures and the general paraphernalia of a lab, sinks and fume cupboards, glassware and balances and labelled bottles, a familiar world without ghosts.

From the beginning there were young colleagues working with Uffer, sometimes on hints from earlier unpublished and sometimes unfinished papers which my father had stuck into a drawer and not gone back to because the immediate work he was on had become so fascinating. Rob Makgill sorted them out with Douglas, Priestley, and Mavro, all young, with my father as S.P.—the Senior Partner. I don't know what the economic basis of all this was. Perhaps the University provided some finance but I don't know. That wasn't talked about. There are still masses of unsorted Haldane papers. One day—but it was the scientific excitement that came through most to my brother with a small spill-over to me.

I was expected to understand more or less what was going on and to take it seriously. There was something very heartening about the study, with its incredible litter of papers spreading from a great central oak table over the floor, and yet Uffer could usually lay hands on what he wanted. It all seemed to have a purpose. Sometimes I went in and there would be an opportune moment to ask questions, sometimes not. What mattered was never measured by a money standard; it was an idea spreading out to new conclusions, it was devising a piece of apparatus, it was convincing the Admiralty, the Home Office, the Institute of Mining Engineers or whatever it might be that something had to be done. It was a saving and bettering of human life.

Yet for me outside that there were huge areas of fantasy. The builders of the new house had left piles of gravelly sand. Here I made roads and railways and towns. Sometimes I found a stone which was in some way special. Perhaps it would become the focus of one of the constructions. It all appeared to be very important, though it would never have gone into a diary. Did the grown-ups think it was all a waste of time? One doesn't know. I remember a calm happiness about this; presumably I was playing God. As perhaps one is when one is assembling a book.

XV

Celebrations and Shows

It was certainly 'Mafeking Night'—popular celebrations for the relief of Mafeking in May 1900. My mother was an ardent imperialist, my father a pro-Boer. The Africans themselves didn't come into it one way or the other. At two and a half none of this affected me. I think Maya must have wanted me to remember this wonderful moment all my life—as indeed, in a way, I have. We were in a crowd which was probably by today's standards sufficiently orderly and gentle, although some of the crowd's methods of rejoicing brought a new word into the English vocabulary—mafficking. No doubt my hand was firmly grasped but for a moment I somehow escaped. Probably for less than a minute but I remember the feeling of sudden freedom, losing myself among strangers' legs. And that is all I do remember.

Boy and I tended to be taken to celebrations, lengthy and decorative Oxford ones, but usually with ices. After I went to school I got into the ice-eating competitors' ranks and once, in Eights Week I expect, won with fourteen. They were pink strawberry and probably smaller than today's, though perhaps made with real fruit and cream. I know I was taken later to various public occasions, royal funerals and coronations, flags and illuminations, crowds watched from windows. Nothing remains except my father telling me that the new neon lights were dangerous. And those crowds. Yes, I liked them. But I enjoyed much more going out from the cousin's house where we were staying in London and playing Indians in Campden Hill Square garden with no grown-ups about.

An important Oxford celebration was the yearly Encaenia. This was supposed to be good for my Latin and also my knowledge of the fairly famous: Empire builders were pointed out. But I only liked the gowns. What did improve my Latin were the carol services at New College which I really did enjoy; there was always a lovely theatrical feeling about them.

However, the main Oxford festivity was Eights Week, walking down through beautiful Christ Church and the meadows, hopping in anticipation, then the barge and how long till the first pink ice? One crowded to the edge, peering over, hoping one would see a boat overturned or some incident on the towpath. Everyone was cheerful, full of Eights Week gossip, what bumps were likely. This being the College barge, I was assumed to be safe, so nobody kept grabbing me. Then came the start, the wait till one could see and hear the first of the race, and almost at once one could start yelling oneself, occasionally for some crew which was doing well or with which one felt some kind of alliance, but rising to the climax of 'Well rowed, New College!' when our own boat shot past, usually well up on the cards which one filled in for the bumps. Then the runners on the towpath going by, the bicycles and the megaphones and the exciting wait for the final results.

The British Medical *soirée* in the Oxford museum was very enjoyable; there were experiments laid on, new types of apparatus and photographs. In Jack's 1904 diary—but Naomi was too young to go that year!—it was great fun: 'My pater was showing a new portable gas analysis apparatus and an apparatus for measuring dust and photographs illustrating miners' phthisis in Cornwall.' Also, after the show the high frequency current machine was made to make sparks. Later *soirées* which I remember were full of equally enthralling things.

The Edinburgh Festival was far in the future and also, I suppose, the fireworks on Calton Hill. There was of course the Auchterarder flower show, when I didn't win a prize for the best bunch of flowers, though mine had more different kinds that anyone else's. But it was all right because Granniema agreed that my bunch was the best and I think gave me a consolation prize.

The early diaries have long and careful descriptions of shows of various kinds to which Boy and I were taken. Sometimes these remind me of what had almost been forgotten, sometimes not a memory trace has been left. The earliest is 1904, when we all, including Sina, my nurse, went to see Buffalo Bill in Edinburgh, after having lunch at Jenner's, an event in itself. There was trick-shooting, the lassooing of a 'horse-thief', rough riders and Red Indians. And then the sideshows with a tiny little lady, another 'with an alive snake round her neck' and above all the performing cockatoos with their castle—yes, I think this does just come back, rather grubby white cockatoos.

It comes back more when I read Jack's diary, increasingly badly written every year. He details the Jenner's lunch: 'strawberries, sugar & cream, scones & lemon squash'. He too liked the lady snake charmer, but also mentioned a giant and a dwarf—Princess Noumahawa. He describes twenty-two different scenes and goes into technical detail about the military ones, but with a certain fine contempt for Yankee methods. There seem also to have been English cavalry, Mexicans, Arabs and Japanese, as well as a replica of the battle of Little Big Horn.

The next year we went to Hengler's Royal Italian Circus: 'I am going to tell only about the performances I was interested in.' These were all animals, including a baby elephant, 'the smallest ever seen in Europe'. After the circus 'we went behind the scenes and fed the beasts'. This was clearly just one better than the Zoo.

The same year we went to Earl's Court, where there must have been some kind of permanent show, where we went on board 'the cruiser' with moving pictures at each side. Then there was the moving staircase—strange to think how unknown this was!—and a diver in a tank: 'very interesting because father is going to Portsmouth to help the Admiralty divers to find out how to work at lower levels.' Last and best was the water chute, something I still love.

This was just before my father took Boy to work with him on his first serious set of experiments: 'Father said he was better than a laboratory boy, he made soda-lime.' We stayed with the Harcourts at their huge house, St Clair, Ryde, and had peaches after breakfast. Vernon Harcourt, the distinguished old chemist, had been one of my father's predecessors as a Gas Referee: he was an FRS of the generation who still had private laboratories for their own work.

Here I was allowed to blow my first glass, undeterred by Sina. Like most really good scientists, Vernon Harcourt was always ready to explain things, even to a child.

Sina and I stayed on at the Seaview Hotel from which I wrote: 'I went to Seaview pier this afternoon, it is a sort of suspension pier, it wiggles when several people go along it.' I have a notion that it also wiggled when firmly jumped upon by me.

We used to go from Cloan to an occasional fair or market, at one of which my mother, nodding to an auctioneer friend, inadvertently bought a flock of lambs. And we went to the library at Innerpeffray where they keep Montrose's sword and Bible, to be shown to and handled by relations, of whom I was one, through descent from Montrose's sister married to a Haldane. That gave one a great feeling of status. Yet I found industrial processes equally fascinating; the day Colonel Hally took us round the Auchterarder cloth mill gets four pages of diary, though I confessed to not quite understanding every bit of the process.

I don't think I now remember anything about the Edinburgh International Exhibition, but at ten I found it deeply satisfactory. 'First we did all the whirligigs, the figure of eight railway, the water chute and the flying boats; then we did the maze.' There were also Jacobite relics, communion tickets and 'a village of West Africans from Sierra Leone. They were very black and horribly ugly. They ran on a far flatter foot than a European and they kicked up their legs in front of them.' They were all doing something, a woman was twisting up her hair into braids 'which looked just like very old boot laces'. The men who were dancing 'were evidently witch doctors'. So much for the imperial point of view! The second day we went to the Exhibition it seems that the main attraction was pictures: 'Some of them were very interesting to me, as I have seen their engravings so often.'

In 1909 we went to the Marine Gardens at Portobello, where there were switchbacks, a roller-skating rink and, best of all, a menagerie with three baby lions, the first to be born in Edinburgh. There was also a small circus with performing animals. Finally tea at a public house managed by the East of Scotland Public House

Trust. The publican got no profit on his alcohol sales, only on the food sales; clearly this interested me; I had already seen too many drunks in Scotland. We seem to have had a very good tea.

As the years go by, while my brother became more deeply interested in science, I seem to be more stirred by visual beauty, storms and sunsets: 'a golden sunset with the Forth Bridge looking like spider's web hung across it'. I was ten when Uncle Richard got a car for Cloan, a Daimler, I expect, and)f course with a driver. My great treat was sitting in front next to him with everything pouring by. There were still flocks of sheep which were quite un-used to motor traffic and ran in front without trying to get away. But there were also children playing Last Over, a game which must have accounted for a few accidents. One day we drove right across the strath to Loch Earn. I write: 'Loch Earn is about the most beautiful place I have ever seen; the further end was hidden by a golden haze, so that it looked unended as if it was the sea.' All was made still better by the Stuarts of Ard Vorlich who showed me their black fantails 'iridescent with green and purple'. Colour and form had begun to beat on me, to need to be written about.

Of course the best show of all was St Giles' Fair at Oxford, though we were not often back from Scotland in time for it. In 1907 'first Boy and I went on a merry-go-round for which they only charged $\frac{1}{2}$ penny, but it was not much fun, but the next one was splendid as the horses went up and down as well as round and round. We went up the lighthouse and slid down again on a mat.' Then we and the Slessors went on the great wheel and after that the whole family engaged in shooting, which must have been rather fairer in those days as 'Mother and I got a bottle down almost every time.' In the end 'Mother went home and Boy and I went to some more shows.'

Although the later diaries found me in Scotland, I had over the years several more days of St Giles' Fair, which have coalesced. One year they started whirling platforms which centrifuged people off. However I managed to stay in the middle, shutting my eyes and carefully spreading my weight in different directions; this impressed the proprietor so much that I got several free rides. We usually came back with coconuts and probably other 'prizes'; the cost of anything was still in pennies and still the top of the great wheel showed the glorious crowded streets and the fair noises coming up, mixed and transmuted. It seems to me, but I may be wrong, that the fair folk were friendlier than they are now, interested not only in collecting the money, but in helping everyone to have a good time.

For me, however, the supreme show seems to have been soldiers. Now, I get this out of the diaries. Otherwise I am sure I would have forgotten it, which only shows what tricks one's subconscious can get up to if one's political convictions are allowed to interfere. I have forgotten quite a number of large areas of imagination, of which army manoeuvres, something very far removed from real life, is one. The other which I know about but cannot get a clue onto which I can latch, is the vast area of stories told to myself which I know went on for years and finally turned into writing story books. There is of course nothing about this in the diaries; it was no part of the outside world. It was as secret as They. But why can't I remember it? Especially as it must have been very much a major part of the Me who is still Me. I think, but with no real certainty, that the stories had no real background in time or place and that they involved long conversations which gave me great pleasure to devise; some may have risen out of the books I read; it is also possible that some may have been a dip into a changed state of consciousness. If this was so, it is quite possible that I might not remember unless I could get back into that particular 'high'. I would not like to be definite about this, but certainly I could get somewhere, so to speak, else, and might have to be recalled and told I was dreaming.

I think sometimes I involved other people in the stories, especially in recognisable activities like the 'orchid-collecting' which gradually merged into the daylight world of real field botany. Boy or my mother might be someone in the story as well as themselves. But what zones of fancy I wandered in and whether—as is probable—they were erotic zones, that door is shut. I may have had fantasies of war, violence, torture, Mazeppa bound on wild horses, but all completely unreal and ready to vanish with my first knowledge of real war and, in the surgical wards of St Thomas's, real wounds and real, stinking gangrene.

That, then, has gone, unless some chance turning over of a stone leaves it uncovered. But the soldiers? There were Territorial camps near Cloan, and an occasional mention in the diaries; but I remember how exciting it was to see the tents and the fires and all the paraphernalia of soldiering. In 1907, in London, 'We passed a battery of Royal Horse Artillery with 6 guns. They looked splendid.' Then there were the O.T.C. camps which Boy clearly enjoyed as he grew older and tougher; they were full of physical tests which he tended to pass with pride and pleasure. But in 1909, in my last but one year at school, we ran into some big army manoeuvres and I write page after excited page. My mother was deep in it; her involvement with army matters and people is clear from her own book.

The diary gets tremendously detailed and excited. They seem to have been the biggest manoeuvres ever to take place in England and it sounds as though everyone had enjoyed them vastly. Boy and I went to the camp at Wolvercote, and two days later the whole family drove out beyond Woodstock. We nearly found ourselves in a flower and dog show and I remark smugly, 'I wonder anyone could go and see a flower show with troops so near.' Soon we found the Gordon Highlanders playing football and some field artillery drawn by cart horses, as well as telephone mules with the coils of wire. The next day we went in another direction, hiring a pony cart at Kingham, and delightedly watched a 'white' scout being captured by the 'browns'. 'Boy, whom we met afterwards, told us that he had seen a man captured by some Highlanders. He had managed to escape, but one of the Highlanders took the safety pin out of his kilt and punctured both tyres of his bicycle, which he had left behind him. Boy lent him some rubber solution to mend the tyres with after the Highlander had gone.'

Then we climbed Ickham Hill and listened excitedly to the rifle fire, 'the pop-popping of the pompoms and the distant roar of big guns'. Boy and I came close to the artillery and watched the whole process. Then there was a battle for Ickham station attacked by the 'whites' and defended by the Gordons. 'They charged down hill into the whites and took about a dozen prisoners. They often got very excited, especially at close quarters, and I saw one man pull his officer down into the ditch beside him, saying "You're not out of their fire, Sir". Altogether I think this was about the nicest day I have had yet. I found *Senecio Erucifolius*, rare.'

That night Boy slept under a hedge and had brambles, chocolate and cider for breakfast 'as the troops had eaten everything else'. The next morning we were out there again, but it was foggy, and I was, I think, a little disappointed to see lancers in their ordinary khaki service clothes 'without pennons on their lances or any of the usual colour on their horses' harness or their own clothes. They looked very businesslike and real.' The next day there was a tremendous hailstorm. I write about the havoc in the garden, and note, 'I am collecting the seeds of the thorn apple in the garden, which can be made into stuff nearly as valuable as opium.' However I think I was aware that it was highly poisonous. I did a lot of experimenting in those days, nibbling away at various plants and occasionally finding something which did me no good. But later the family went off again to look at the soaked troops; I think: 'it must be terribly unwholesome work lying out in the wet all night'. The diary ends with the same smug note: 'We seem to have seen more of the manoeuvres than most civilians.'

This was the diary which, on another page, records that I had been 'reading More's "Utopia" as you advised me'—this no doubt being pointed at the Skipper! 'It strikes me as being a most horribly socialistic place, where it would be impossible to live in peace.' A rather odd comment.

But why, until I looked at the diaries again, had I so totally forgotten the manoeuvres? I suppose all that was completely blotted out by real war, the first excitement almost like manoeuvres, imagined as being the same, except that the British army seemed inexplicably to be retreating. And then the repeated shock of the killings when one after the other of my friends were killed—gone for always—and I went to Nigg to see Boy in the Black Watch and knew I would do anything in the world to avert it from him but knew also that I was utterly powerless to do anything at all.